Praise for Pain-Free Dental Deals

Bill Barrett and his legal team aren't just my attorneys. They act as a legal department within my company. Their experience, knowledge, and contacts, we were able to grow from a family company to a mid-size corporation within a couple of years. They helped us navigate and avoid business pitfalls while accelerating our growth and improving our success. Their role in our organization is indispensable.

—M. Elder, DDS, MD
California

In our experience, finding the right attorney is like finding the right dentist. You're looking for someone who takes the time to understand the full situation, and then takes the time to explain the recommended course of action that keeps me safe but also addresses what's most important to us as the client or patient. We've had the privilege of working with Bill, Casey, and many more at Mandelbaum Barrett PC on a number of different legal areas as our practice has grown, and the experience has been fantastic. We're currently working on our first practice merger with Bill and Casey. As owners, we have so many questions, so it's comforting to know that the legal team on our side has enough first-hand experience to give us advice we can trust and resources to get our questions answered.

—Dee Dee Meevasin, DMD, and Michael Cruz
Nevada

We've been honored to be a client of Bill Barrett's for many years. Bill is considered one of the top dental business advisors in the country. We've engaged Bill and his team as our trusted business advisors and consultants for our private group dental practice in NYC. As our practice has grown and changed with the times, Bill and his team have been there to navigate and advise us through a variety of complex business matters. He and his team are professional, organized, and focused on the task at hand, all the while ensuring that we implement the most optimal strategic plans of action.

—Dr. Howard J. Spielman, DDS
New York

I started working with Bill and Casey during a critical time in my career. My partner of ten years was retiring, and there were so many issues that we needed to work through. Bill and Casey did an amazing job of navigating the minefield of issues and came to the best solutions possible. I can't imagine how bad it could've been without them. I have continued my relationship with them, and we've since gone through several acquisitions. Their expertise and guidance have been priceless. I'm so grateful I found them, and I've thoroughly enjoyed working with both of them.

—Dr. Joseph Field
California

Bill and Casey have guided me through a practice acquisition, a partial sale of a practice, and a practice fold-in, as well as various associate contracts. We've completed the full circle of a practice's life and more, and we're only getting started. I can't think of anyone I would rather have to help me through the process and I highly recommend them to others as well.

—Dr. Aaron Rauen
Iowa

I was originally introduced to Mandelbaum Barrett PC through Fortune Practice Management, a business coaching company for dentists, to assist me with the development of a DSO. Over the last ten years, I've experimented with other firms, but I immediately knew that Mandelbaum was the firm I'd been looking for. At the end of 2018, Bill and Casey were not only able to execute but also provided high-level strategic advice for me to complete numerous major business deals to launch me into 2019. This consisted of two merger acquisitions of other practices, a real estate purchase, a dental lab startup, formation of the "C"-level team, and the sale of a portion of my DSO to a new partner. Having a team of professionals that can support my growth needs as well as help to guide and narrate specific business goals is a must for anyone serious about business growth and development! A great guide to doing it right the first time!

—Curtis Crandall
Pennsylvania

Bill Barrett continues to exceed our expectations and is an incredible legal advocate for our business. Not only does his firm provide professional win–win legal strategies, but they also support and promote our entrepreneurial leadership. Bill always has a supportive and thoughtful response as well as fresh ideas to contribute. His dedication to excellence is a pleasure and inspiration.

—Dr. Greg Shelhouse
Ohio

I met Bill pretty early in both of our careers. He was representing the party with whom I was negotiating. . . . As I sat there across the table from him, it was clear I was outmatched. It was then I knew there wouldn't be anyone else I'd allow to represent my interests. Then, I met Casey. The experience and insight they each brought to the table in every deal I've done gives me confidence that I have the right team on my side for every deal to come.

—Jason M. Auerbach, DDS
New Jersey

Casey was tremendous in my initial acquisition with my business partner. She was supportive and accommodating throughout the process, educating us on the good and bad parts of a contract. Her knowledge in the field allowed us to make an educated decision. It's clear that she has a desire to help and assist with good intention. I highly recommend this firm for legal services—you'll be happy you made the choice.

—Lewis Chen, DDS
New York

Bill and Casey are the two most impressive professionals with whom we've ever worked. I suppose they've spoiled us, or perhaps they make all their clients feel as safe and protected as they make us feel. I love when patients complain about attorneys because it's an opportunity to brag about mine. These two lawyers become part of your executive team, take pride in your success, and revel in the benefits of a well-counseled organization. We couldn't be more thankful to have found such wonderful people and advisors.

—Gary Silverstrom, DDS
New Jersey

PAIN FREE

AN ENTREPRENEURIAL DENTIST'S GUIDE TO BUYING, SELLING, AND MERGING PRACTICES

DENTAL DEALS

WILLIAM S. BARRETT

WITH CASEY GOCEL

ethos
collective

Printed in the United States of America

Published by Ethos Collective™
PO Box 43, Powell, OH 43065
ethoscollective.vip

LCCN: 2021901743

ISBN: 978-1-63680-023-3 (paperback)
ISBN: 978-1-63680-024-0 (hardback)
ISBN: 978-1-63680-025-7 (ebook)

Available in paperback, hardback, ebook, and audiobook

Any Internet addresses (websites, blogs, etc.) and telephone numbers printed in this book are offered as a resource. They are not intended in any way to be or imply an endorsement by Ethos Collective, nor does Ethos Collective vouch for the content of these sites and numbers for the life of this book.

Some names and identifying details have been changed to protect the privacy of individuals.

CONTENTS

FOREWORD

I first met Bill Barrett five years ago, when he and I were asked to join the Advisory Board of Fortune Management's Fortune 50, a group that provides training for entrepreneurial dentists who want to supercharge their businesses. A lot has changed since then, but two things endure—Bill's innate feel for the market and his ability to steer even the hairiest deal to a successful close.

The dentists we work with today are savvier than ever, as are their patients. Like consumers in many other industries, modern dental patients want what they want, and they want it now. In response, dentists have had to make great strides in customer service—providing flexible operating hours, online booking, a frictionless experience, general and specialty dentistry under one roof, and many other bells and whistles of today's on-demand culture. The result is a new generation of dentists who think like entrepreneurs and understand the power of scaling their businesses like never before.

It's my honor to pen the foreword for this premier book for dental practitioners who want to elevate their game from chairside practitioner to successful entrepreneur. Bill's well-grounded grasp of deal mechanics and the business of dentistry is evident throughout, and his advice on buying, selling, and merging practices is specifically written with you in mind. So find a comfortable spot, and expect to dog-ear pages as you discover the pain-free path forward for your next dental deal.

—Fred Joyal
Speaker, Author, Dental Marketing Expert, Entrepreneur

AN INVITATION

TO THE DENTIST ABOUT TO DO A DEAL

If you've picked up this book, you're probably considering entering into a business transaction involving a dental or dental specialty practice. Congratulations! This is a very exciting time!

If you're thinking of buying, selling, merging, or contemplating a partnership transaction, this book was written for you. Whether this is your first deal or you're an entrepreneurial dentist with many deals under your belt, the purpose of this book is to help you navigate the process of closing a dental practice transaction in the most effective, ethical, and successful manner possible.

My name is Bill Barrett, and I'm the CEO of Mandelbaum Barrett PC, a full-service law firm that has been serving clients since 1930. When I joined the firm twenty years ago, a member of the Academy of Dental CPAs introduced me to the dental profession, and I had the opportunity to work with several dentists.

As I started to learn the business and profession of dentistry, I became increasingly aware that the dental community was often poorly served by their legal representation; critical deal terms were frequently overlooked. Dentists were entering into agreements that affected their careers and financial lives, not to mention their team members' and patients' lives, with relatively poor guidance. Because these dentists were turning to advisors who lacked a deep understanding of the nuances involved in dental practice transactions, many were unknowingly creating significant problems for themselves—financial problems, tax problems, personnel problems, and legal problems— which became glaringly apparent after the closing.

When I saw this void in representation and legal services, I was inspired to create a practice area within our law firm that would endeavor to become the national standard for the representation of dentists and dental specialists in business transactions throughout the country. And with that, our law firm's National Dental Law Group at Mandelbaum Barrett PC was born.

I wanted the Dental Law Center to be a place where dentists could receive the highest quality of legal services and have full confidence that they were working with attorneys who understood every aspect of a dental practice transaction, whether the client was an associate buying into a practice for the first time or a sophisticated dentist– entrepreneur creating a structure for the ownership and management of multiple practices.

I've spent the last two decades building the Dental Law Center and recruiting the top talent in the legal profession to assist me. To date, we've successfully closed several hundred dental and dental specialist transactions nationwide.

This book is the culmination of our team's many years of experience. It addresses not only the "how-to" aspect of closing a transaction but also the pitfalls to avoid when navigating the process.

Throughout my career, I've learned many valuable lessons about successful (and not-so-successful) dental transactions. My goal in writing this book is to share these true stories and experiences with you, so you can avoid making mistakes that others (including me) have made in the past.

There has never been a better time to invest in the dental profession. Bank financing is readily available, and the continued emergence of dental service organizations (DSOs) and corporate dentistry investment has added yet another interesting twist to the marketplace. Dentists are more entrepreneurial than ever, and the opportunities are endless. As you read this book, you'll learn the *rules of the road* for navigating these transactions the right way.

If you've ever heard the expression, "Measure twice; cut once," you understand that it's always best to do your homework before taking action. At the Dental Law Center, we've done all the measuring, and we've seen all the mistakes, as well as wonderful success stories. I hope that after reading this book, you'll become excited about the possibilities that exist for you as an entrepreneurial dentist. You'll understand exactly how to do your homework, and you'll be ready to take action.

Let's get started!
—William Barrett, Esq.

CHAPTER 1

BUYING, SELLING, OR MERGING A DENTAL PRACTICE: WHAT TO EXPECT

Stop being afraid of what could go wrong, and start being excited about what could go right.

—Tony Robbins

Perhaps you're a seasoned dentist looking to sell your practice as part of your exit strategy. Or maybe you're an entrepreneurial dentist interested in expanding and purchasing more practices. Or you could be reading this book because you're an associate who wishes to buy into an existing practice. Whatever your reason, I'm here to help you navigate the complexities of these transactions (known in the industry as "practice transitions") while avoiding some of the costly mistakes I've seen in my twenty-plus years of practice.

As you read on, you'll learn about some often over-looked, misunderstood, and even ignored considerations when purchasing, selling, or merging dental practices. I've seen it all, and I'm here to guide you through this exciting time.

Let's look at an example. Samantha Sanders, DDS, is about to make the biggest decision of her life. She is selling her practice to her dental school classmate, Dan Daniels, DDS. They've known each other forever and have referred patients to each other for more than a decade. Samantha is even godmother to Dan's two children. Because of their close relationship, they've decided they don't need to get a lawyer involved in their transaction. Instead, they've hired a practice broker to handle the whole deal. They believe it's simpler and far more cost-effective. What could go wrong?

We see deals like this all the time. In this example, let's assume that Samantha and Dan hire a great broker. He negotiates the best possible price and terms and presents a contract that he considers neutral. Samantha and Dan are happy with the deal, and both agree to sign the contract. However, as the closing date approaches, things begin to unravel.

Two weeks before the closing, Samantha meets with her landlord to inform him that Dan will be taking over the practice and the lease. Samantha has always had a great relationship with her landlord, but this time, things don't seem so cordial. Her landlord informs her that she doesn't have the right to assign her lease to Dan. Although the landlord is willing to consider an assignment, it'll be conditioned on his review of Dan's financials and Dan's willingness to give a personal guarantee. In addition, the landlord reminds Samantha that she gave a personal guarantee that will continue even if the lease is assigned to Dan. Needless to say, Samantha is surprised by this news.

Later that week, Samantha and Dan meet for lunch. Dan casually asks Samantha what she plans to do after the closing. Samantha beams as she tells Dan about her new job at a local cosmetic practice.

"What do you mean?" Dan asks. "I thought you were retiring."

"Yes, that was my original plan," Samantha explains, "but I've been offered a wonderful opportunity at Brilliant Smiles Cosmetic Dentistry. They're looking for someone to perform general dentistry only one day a week. So, I'll be able to continue practicing on a limited basis."

Dan does his best to remain calm, but he can feel the anger rising as he reminds Samantha that she is bound by a five-year non-compete clause.

"I know," Samantha replies, "but Brilliant Smiles is actually seven miles away, so I assumed you wouldn't mind."

Dan is furious. It never occurred to him to check the distance of the non-compete clause because he thought Samantha was retiring.

In this example, these issues arose before the closing of the transaction. This means that there may still be time to fix the problems and save the

> I've seen these types of scenarios play out over and over again, and often conflicts don't arise until the deal is done.

deal. However, I've seen these types of scenarios play out over and over again, and often conflicts don't arise until the deal is done. Dentists who were once the best of friends become bitter enemies.

Let's go back to our example and assume that Dan and Samantha sign and close their transaction without any preclosing hurdles. Dan happily operates the practice in the weeks following the closing, and as she promised, Samantha comes into the office several hours a day to assist with the transition. Initially, everything seems fine. But as weeks turn to months, a trend begins to emerge.

Patients are regularly presenting with complaints of poor dentistry that needs to be repaired. The first two times it happens, Dan graciously agrees to perform the corrective treatment at his expense. But as two cases turn into twenty cases, Dan realizes that Samantha has a long history of performing subpar dentistry.

Dan struggles with how to handle this. First, there's nothing in the contract to address who'll pay for corrective treatment. Second, he doesn't want to ask Samantha to perform the work, because it's clear that she doesn't have the required skill. He also doesn't think that he should have to bear the expense of her mistakes. Ultimately, Dan feels compelled to make the patients happy—because if he doesn't, he'll lose their future business. Dan spends the next three months fixing all of Samantha's mistakes at his cost.

After the closing, Dan finally focuses on the fact that Samantha has more than $200,000 in outstanding receivables. According to the contract, the accounts receivables belong to Samantha and must be collected on a "first-in, first-out" basis. In other words, any payment from a patient must be applied to the oldest invoice. This didn't seem like a big deal to Dan when he signed the contract, because he failed to discover that her receivables were so high. Now that he's trying to run the business, he's struggling with a serious cash-flow problem because most of the money coming into the practice is being paid out to Samantha for past-due amounts.

These are only a few examples of issues we've encountered when advising dentists. The lesson here is clear: When engaging in a dental practice transaction, both parties need to hire an attorney with expertise in dentistry. I know what you're thinking: Lawyers cost a lot of money and cause many problems. I get it. I've heard all the stereotypes, and unfortunately, I know a few lawyers who exemplify them. But not all lawyers are the same, and the good ones save you money and prevent problems.

Not all lawyers are the same, and the good ones save you money and prevent problems.

I wrote this book to help entrepreneurial dentists like yourself understand what can go wrong, so you can take the required steps to ensure that your deal goes right. I want you to walk away with an in-depth understanding of all facets of any dental practice transaction you enter into. The dental community is underserved and underrepresented by the legal industry. I want to help you navigate a successful practice transition that protects you, your family, your finances, your patients, and your professional future.

Read on, and let's discuss the pitfalls and the many opportunities available when you buy, sell, or merge a dental practice.

CHAPTER 2

DUE DILIGENCE: WHAT ARE YOU ACTUALLY BUYING (OR SELLING)?

Sweat equity is the most valuable equity there is.
Know your business and industry better than
anyone else in the world.

—Mark Cuban

The process of buying or selling a dental practice is complicated and time-consuming. However, if done correctly, the result can (and should) be a successful transaction for both parties. The first step in every successful dental practice transition is conducting due diligence. Due diligence is a fancy term that professionals use. It may sound complicated, but it's quite simple: Due diligence is best defined as doing your homework. To quote my good friend and Fortune Management CEO, Bernie Stoltz, we're looking for a "win-win strategy."

The purpose of conducting due diligence is to avoid making mistakes that may cost you time and money in the future. We understand the desire to close a deal quickly, but a failure to conduct proper due diligence before signing a contract can result in disaster. Ninety percent of the problems triggered by failed transactions could have been avoided if only the participants had done their homework first.

Ninety percent of the problems triggered by failed transactions could have been avoided if only the participants had done their homework first.

Both the buyer and the seller should perform due diligence. For example, a seller's due diligence will involve a comprehensive review of the practice's value to ensure she gets the best possible purchase price. On the other hand, a buyer will also want to review the financials to make sure he doesn't overpay.

There are several different types of due diligence, which I'll discuss in detail later in this chapter, but the first step of the process is to assemble your team.

Assembling Your "Board of Directors"

Having a transactional attorney conversant in dental practices is critical to your success, but it takes more than one professional to vet a good deal properly. It takes an entire team of dental practice transaction specialists to ensure you enter into the best possible contract. Think of your transaction team as your board of directors.

Think of your transaction team as your board of directors.

Accountant

The first member of your team—and one of the most important—is your accountant. When engaging in a transaction, you must have an accountant who specializes in dentistry. This is vital when it comes to valuing the practice, assessing patient receivables, and scrutinizing the practice's tax returns. Do the numbers add up? Is everything as it appears? A good dental accountant can save you from making a six-figure mistake; he or she can uncover fraud, overbilling, or receivable issues hidden in the numbers. Is your accountant only someone who prepares your taxes, or can he or she get under the hood of a dental practice and understand what's going on with cash flow, assets and liabilities, and the percentages of revenue derived from different procedures?

A good accountant will conduct chart audits to make sure that the numbers on the balance sheet match up with the work that's being performed and billed to insurance carriers. The only time you should ever learn about fraudulent financial conduct is *before* entering into a deal.

Attorney

The second member of your team is a dental practice transactional attorney. Again, the key here is to hire a specialist. Lawyers come in all different shapes and sizes. We have different price points and different specialties. Throughout the transaction process, your lawyer will be your biggest ally and your closest friend. You should hire someone whom you trust and enjoy working with. It's also important to remember that a lawyer who spends most of the day on trials probably doesn't have as much transaction experience. A lawyer who doesn't have experience with dental practice transitions probably won't uncover important issues that are specific to dental practices, such as corrective treatment, work in progress, and the appropriate structure of the transition period. If your brother happens to be a divorce attorney and offers to help you sell your practice, you may want to consider asking for a referral to a dental practice transaction specialist.

Broker

Not every transaction involves a practice broker. A broker is a third party whom sellers often hire to market a practice and find a suitable buyer. Sometimes, buyers also hire a broker to search for a target practice to be acquired. A broker experienced in the dental community, and specifically in the geography you're targeting, can be an excellent resource not only in putting a deal together but also in helping the parties reach an equitable and fair deal. Just like accountants and attorneys, not all brokers are created equal, and we highly recommend working with a broker who has experience in the dental community.

A broker's job is, first and foremost, to identify the parties. This is why brokers are typically hired even before the lawyers and accountants get involved. An ideal practice broker will help negotiate deal terms, assist with due diligence, and guide you through the entire process. Picking a good broker is a bit like hiring a marketing consultant. You want someone who's going to make you look your best.

Dental Practice Management Consultant

In assembling your team, you should also consider engaging a top-notch dental practice management consultant. A dental practice management consultant can help you take the pulse of the practice. For example, let's assume the practice has five thousand patients on the books, and you ask the consultant to do a deeper dive. The dental practice management consultant can determine how many of those patients are *current* patients, and how many haven't been seen in years. The consultant can also tell you who's coming in, how often, and what type of treatment is being proposed and provided. It isn't uncommon for practice buyers to be so caught up in the emotion and haste of closing a deal that they neglect the critical step of understanding what's going on from a treatment perspective.

Practice management consultants are also skilled at understanding the culture of a practice and the staff's personalities. What is the office manager like? How good is the receptionist? Do the hygienists have a good rapport with the patients? Does the office live up to the claims that the seller is making? Are salaries in line with market norms, or do they exceed them owing to a large number of legacy relationships? Consultants also can map out the post-closing enhancements you'll need to consider to take the practice to the next level.

Banker

If you're a buyer and need financing, another key member of your board of directors is your banker. At the risk of sounding like a broken record, I will state, once again, that your banker should be specialized in dental practice transactions.

Many wonderful financing programs are available specifically for dentists. Dental practice transaction bankers understand the inner workings of a practice and how the cash flow works. As a result, it isn't unheard of for a bank to offer a young practice buyer 100 percent financing. The dental lending community offers many other great opportunities if you're working with the right bank.

Another plus to working with a bank is that the bank will do its own due diligence. Bank officials will review your lease and purchase agreements. Banks want to invest in solid practices, and the result is that an extra set of advisors will review your documents to make sure you're getting a great deal. Banks want to confirm that the length of your lease is adequate and that the terms of your purchase agreement are reasonable, customary, and fair. Most importantly, they will value the practice to ensure that you aren't overpaying and they aren't over-lending.

The bank's due diligence may seem like a hassle while you're going through it, but it's a huge benefit to you as the borrower. Establishing a relationship with a good bank early on can be crucial to your long-term success. In the future, you may need your banker for an equipment loan, a line of credit, a real estate purchase, or even a future practice acquisition. I often caution dentists to look for the best long-term relationship, not simply the lowest current interest rate.

Sometimes, when I advise putting together a board of directors like this, clients resist because they don't want to spend the time and money. I understand; nobody likes to spend money unnecessarily, especially on intangibles such as advice and guidance. However, time and money invested in thorough due diligence now can yield significant savings later. Ultimately, you'll spend a lot less money engaging professionals before a transaction than you'd spend on the forensic accountants or litigation attorneys you'd have to hire if issues weren't discovered in a timely manner. It's like that old muffler ad, where the salesman says, "You can pay me now, or you can pay me later." You'd be well served by paying a little to have a great team, a smooth transaction, and a deal in which everyone walks away with a positive result.

It's Time to Do Your Homework

Now that you have your team in place, it's time to acquire a thorough understanding of what type of practice you're buying. As I mentioned before, there are many types of due diligence. The most common are financial review, insurance assessment, lien searches, patient analysis, staff personality and culture, and real estate/lease review.

Finances and Insurance

Financial and insurance due diligence is generally something that everyone understands. You must know what you're buying, and you must understand whether the practice is primarily driven by insurance or a fee-for-service practice.

As I discussed in detail earlier, a good accountant will do more than simply value the practice. Financial and insurance due diligence should include a comprehensive analysis of the practice's books, tax returns, accounts receivable, and insurance practices.

If you're reading this book, you're likely an experienced dentist with a good understanding of practice finances and proper billing practices. However, I'd caution you against conducting this type of due diligence yourself. Professional accountants and practice management consultants are trained to pick up on issues that aren't easily discoverable, particularly when the seller (or the staff) has taken intentional steps to hide things they don't want a potential buyer to find.

Lien and Judgment Searches

When representing a buyer, an experienced attorney will always run full lien and judgment searches on the seller. These results can unveil a host of issues that will need to be cleared up before closing, such as outstanding debt on the practice, unpaid equipment leases, and outstanding judgments. To pass clear title of the practice from one owner to the next, all practice debt will need to be paid at closing, and all liens will need to be released. Debt on a practice isn't a problem, so long as the purchase price is high enough to cover all of the seller's liabilities.

Failure to release liens on a practice before consummating a sale can result in something called *successor liability*. This means that the buyer of a practice may become liable for the debts of the seller as a result of taking ownership of assets that weren't legally transferrable. The result of this can be devastating to the buyer. This is why the first order of business in every transaction we handle is to conduct a full lien and judgment search on the seller.

While we're on the topic of successor liability, it's important to note that the use of the seller's practice name after the closing could present potential liability issues for the buyer in certain states.

Just last year, we represented the buyer of a practice. In the purchase agreement, the parties agreed that the buyer would have the right to continue using the seller's practice name after the closing. Several months later, a former employee of the practice (whom the buyer had never met) filed a lawsuit against the seller, but also named the buyer personally as a defendant.

Under state law, the former employee had the right to name the buyer personally; the new owner was forced to defend himself. In this particular state, the law provided that if the buyer continued to use the name of the seller and a reasonable member of the public would think that ownership hadn't changed, then the plaintiff had the right to sue the buyer personally. Fortunately, our agreements were clear that the seller had to indemnify the buyer for this claim, so the buyer was reimbursed for his defense costs.

Patients and Staff Members

Patient analysis and culture assessment are two types of diligence that are often overlooked. Is the practice's culture in line with your vision of how dental patients should be served? If not, could it be transformed into the kind of practice you want to own? It's a question of knowing the "bones" of the practice. Are the team members right for you? Is the direction of the practice compatible with yours? Are the staff and location capable of growing with your vision?

Consider a senior dentist selling a practice that consists primarily of patients over the age of sixty-five. Seniors tend to be terrific patients. They need restoration work; they understand the importance of regular cleanings; and in many cases, they can afford the services required. Purchasing a practice with a high concentration of senior patients will likely result in solid revenue over the next five to ten years.

But what about the future of the practice? How many new patients is the practice adding each year? What is the age demographic of these patients? If a dentist knows that she's winding down her career, she may not put much emphasis on bringing new patients into the practice. The numbers may be solid right now, but if there's no marketing in place to ensure a steady stream of new faces, what will the practice look like five or ten years from now? This is why it's so important to understand the demographics of the patients and not just the numbers on the balance sheet.

When it comes to staffing, the best course of action is to interview all team members before entering into the purchase agreement. Although this is part of the due diligence process, it's often the very last step, because the seller should be comfortable with the deal before allowing the buyer to speak with the employees. When a team hears that a practice is going to be sold, it can be very stressful. Are they going to keep their jobs? Will their hours change? Will salaries and benefits change? Who will be in charge?

As a buyer, your discussions with the staff are vitally important. For one thing, this is your opportunity to reassure your new employees that their positions are secure. This is also a great time to discuss any positive changes that you hope to make to the practice. If you're planning to renovate the office or buy new equipment or new furniture, let your staff know. Anything you can do to bring excitement to the transition will help alleviate fears and create trust.

We recommend that buyers complete all their due diligence (other than the staff interviews) and finalize the most important transaction documents, including the purchase agreement, the lease, and, if applicable, the seller's employment agreement. Next, we'll indicate to the seller that we've signed off on the transaction, and the only remaining item of due diligence is the team meeting. We're basically saying, "Everything else is fine. Assuming the meeting with the team goes well, we have a deal." This is common practice in purchase agreements in almost every industry; buyers will have conversations with key employees and customers before they sign the agreement.

It's natural that a seller won't want the buyer speaking to the staff until she knows that the deal is fully negotiated, contracts are finalized, and all other due diligence items have been completed to the buyer's satisfaction. This is why staff interviews are typically the final step.

Location, Location, Location

There's no question that the location of a practice can have a profound impact on its success and growth potential. Real estate due diligence requires a thorough understanding of the neighborhood and its demographics. This assessment is usually straightforward and can be completed fairly quickly. The harder assessment lies in understanding the details that you can't see.

Buying Real Estate

If your transaction involves the *purchase* of real estate, your due diligence will always include a property inspection and a title search. In some cases, we also advise our clients to get a Phase I Environmental Site Assessment done, just to be certain there are no areas of concern that would require further investigation. One time, a client asked what that'd cost, and we told him it was $2,500 or so, payable to an environmental consulting firm. The client was hesitant to incur this additional cost, and after consulting with his advisors, he told me that no one he spoke with had ever heard of doing an environmental investigation. The client ultimately passed on the environmental study. We reluctantly respected his wishes.

This particular dental practice had an oil tank in the basement that was used to heat the building. As the closing date approached, a local oil company was called out to the property to determine the amount of oil remaining in the tank. This is fairly common practice when selling real estate, because there's an adjustment to the purchase price for any oil that's left in the tank at closing. To make a long story short, the inspector noticed an old pipe in the basement of the house, and it ultimately led to the discovery of a larger underground oil tank on the property. It gets worse. . . .

Workers had to dig up the tank, and when they did, they found contamination. The tank was leaking oil into the ground.

Needless to say, this was a very expensive problem. Our environmental attorneys had to get involved, we were forced to hire an outside environmental consultant, and the tank had to be removed. Because the soil was contaminated, it also had to be removed all the way to a depth at which it was considered clean. The Environmental Protection Agency had to sign off on the whole thing, and the closing was delayed by four months.

Hindsight is always 20/20, and due diligence isn't cheap. But failing to do the proper due diligence will cost you so much more, not to mention wasted time. In this particular case, a leaking oil tank had been underground for fifty years and no one knew about it. What if the environmental contamination had been much worse? What if it hadn't been discovered but was later found to have polluted the groundwater?

If the buyer had done appropriate testing right away, and nothing turned up, he would've been considered an innocent purchaser under the state's laws. But because he failed to do the required analysis, he would've been personally liable for that contamination, and he would've been responsible for having it cleaned up. If you discovered a major issue like this years later, you may have grounds to hold the former owners responsible, but you'd have little chance of collecting damages. The seller may not even be living at that time. In any event, this isn't what you want to be doing when you could be serving your patients or putting time and money into marketing and growing your practice. It's our job and our mission to protect you, and it's always better to address these potential problems now, rather than paying a bigger price down the road.

Leasing Real Estate

If your transaction involves a real estate lease, your due diligence will include a comprehensive legal review of the lease terms. Depending on the outcome of the lease review, the transaction will likely include the negotiation of new lease terms with the property owner, in the form of either an amendment to the existing lease or a completely new agreement.

In the last chapter, we touched briefly on the question of what happens if a lease is problematic. Let's go a little deeper here so you know exactly what to think about and watch for. Let's say the current dentist is a tenant, and we're representing you as the buyer. We're going to have to negotiate a new lease or take assignment of an existing one. Either way, we must understand who owns the property, what the relationship is between the owner and the selling dentist, and what type of lease they have. This is critically important, because if you find a practice that you really like, and it aligns with your vision of where you want to go in your career, you need to be able to answer an important question: Will you be able to keep the location?

The first thing you want to find out, regardless of whether you're the buyer or the seller, is whether the lease provides for an assignment. It can be profoundly disappointing when you spend a lot of time and effort working out a deal with the buyer, only to find out that your lease prohibits assignment.

Typically, leases will allow assignment to a new owner "subject to the lessor's consent." Leases often include clauses that read, "The consent to assign shall not be unreasonably withheld, conditioned, or delayed." A layperson may look at that language and say, "Great, the lessor has to consent to the assignment."

Unfortunately, this isn't always the case. If you were to look at the case law in most states, you would find that "reasonable" can be broadly construed. In other words, things aren't as simple as they seem. For example, property owners are completely within their rights to require the buyer's personal guarantee; in fact, they usually do. They also have the right to review the buyer's financial statements and tax returns to determine whether they think the buyer is as financially strong as the seller. Property owners can also request additional security deposits from the buyer.

The buyer isn't the only one who needs to be concerned here. It's also quite common for the lessor to require the seller to stay on the lease as a personal guarantor even after the sale of the practice has closed. This isn't a matter of simply vouching for your buyer. It means that if the buyer defaults on the lease, the seller is personally responsible for the unpaid rent.

Lease review is one of the most crucial parts of due diligence. The most common cause of delayed and failed dental practice transactions is a failure to adequately review the lease and begin negotiations with the property owner early in the process.

You must know exactly what the lease says, and you must know exactly what your rights and responsibilities are if you're going to sign off on the deal.

We had a recent case in which a dentist sold his practice for about $1.1 million. The terms of the lease were awful, and the property owner took full advantage of the situation. In fact, he demanded that 10 percent of the purchase price be held by his attorney in a trust account as "extra protection just in case there's a default." The owner wanted that money to cover his potential future costs in the event that the buyer broke the lease. He argued he'd need this money to cover his potential future real estate broker commission, the cost of reletting the premises to someone else, upgrading the property . . . and the list went on and on. It was by far the most egregious and unreasonable request I've ever seen from a building owner. Negotiations with this particular owner took four months!

This is why it's so vitally important to begin the due diligence process early, hire the right people, set the wheels in motion, and let your trusted advisors do their jobs.

If you bring your deal to a new attorney days before closing in hopes of getting some last-minute assistance, you'll likely be unhappy with the end result. The reality is that your advisors need adequate time to do their jobs, conduct the proper due diligence, and engage in the necessary negotiations to ensure that you're adequately protected. The lease negotiation alone could be fatal to the buyer's or seller's financial future if not addressed properly.

It isn't my intention to scare dental practice buyers. I'm merely trying to *alert* you to details that need attention. Never let anyone tell you, "Oh, it's just a standard lease," or "It's just boilerplate." From my perspective, there's no such thing. Every word in a lease is in there for a reason, and lessors generally don't include any language that's beneficial to the tenant.

If you plan to get bank financing to purchase the practice, the bank will conduct a thorough review of the lease agreement. The bank's primary concern is to ensure that the term of the lease covers the term of the bank loan. For example, if you're planning to sign a ten-year note with your lender, but your lease only has four years remaining on the term, with no options to renew, the bank will likely require an amendment to the lease as a condition to lending you the purchase price. Specifically, lenders will require a minimum of two options to renew so that they're confident you'll have the ability to operate the practice at its current location for the full ten-year payment term.

On the subject of leases, I'd like to share one final experience. Just last year, we were in the process of negotiating a letter of intent for a merger into our client's location when we received notice from the seller's lessor that the building was going to be demolished. Did you know that in some places, residential values are greater than commercial uses such as office space? In this particular case, the property owner decided to get rid of all the tenants, knock down the building, and develop residential condos. Needless to say, all parties were shocked. The deal died, and our client was forced to relocate her office.

So, if you're thinking of buying a practice, please be sure to have your attorney check to see whether there is a demolition or relocation clause in the lease. A reasonable lease should require at least one year's notice in the event the owner wishes to demolish the building, as well as financial compensation for the costs of relocation.

Local Ordinances

Another issue to consider when buying or leasing real estate is the local laws governing property use. Zoning ordinances, certificates of occupancy, and parking issues can all be catalysts for delaying a transaction.

There's a concept in zoning law called *non-conforming use*. Typically, this means that a particular business was operating in a location before the passage of current zoning laws that now prohibit using the property for that specific purpose. This is particularly common in home-based offices and practices located in residential neighborhoods. The practice you're considering may be permitted to operate as a dental practice because it predated the current law. However, that same law may state that on transfer of ownership, the new owner is no longer allowed to use the property for commercial purposes.

These types of issues are easily overlooked when parties are so eager to get a deal done that they rush the due diligence process. Every municipality has different rules. Zoning is one issue, but certificates of occupancy are another common cause of delay. In some municipalities, a transfer of a certificate of occupancy or the issuance of a new certificate of occupancy for a buyer can trigger a town board meeting to get approval for continued use. Sometimes the sticking point is parking. The buyer will have to testify before the board about future plans for the location—how many dentists and how many patients are expected? Any intended changes can have an impact on the current zoning of the property and can potentially kill the deal.

Addressing these issues before you're at the deal table will increase your chances of success and save you a lot of time.

Associate Buy-ins

The due diligence issues discussed above are important for any type of practice acquisition, but there are a few additional things to consider in the event you're buying only a share in a dental practice. This most often occurs when associate dentists purchase a minority interest (less than 50 percent) in the dental practice where they work.

In these types of transactions, cultural due diligence is supremely important. It's essential to understand the personality of the senior dentist and the culture that's been created with the staff and patients. This likely won't change when you buy into the practice, particularly as a minority owner, so you must make sure it's a good fit. The longer you work for the practice before your buy-in, the more familiar you'll be with the internal dynamics of the office.

I've seen cases in which the senior dentist undercuts the buyer at every turn, even though he has more than $500,000 of the buyer's money in his pocket. The younger dentist will propose a treatment plan to a patient, the patient will go to the senior dentist for advice, and the older dentist will say, "Are you kidding? You don't need that!" Or the new dentist wants to institute new practices and procedures to improve the way the office is run, and the senior dentist covertly tells the office staff, "You don't have to listen to him. I've been doing this for forty years, and we're going to stick to the tried and true."

This sort of undermining can hamper the younger partner's potential. A younger partner has one chance to build trust with the patients and the staff. Without the support of the senior dentist, this is impossible.

Adding a junior partner to an existing practice is a little bit like a marriage. You're going to be, metaphorically speaking, living in the same house with this person. You have to see the world the same way and have the ability to own and manage the practice together.

Here are some other things to consider:

- Is the senior dentist respectful to the staff?
- Is he well-liked by the staff?

- What have you heard about his reputation and personality?
- Is he honest?
- Is he ethical?
- Does he regularly get paid in cash?
- If so, are those transactions properly recorded?

The best way to gauge your prospective partner's personality is to talk to the current patients, staff members, and referral sources. Read the charts. Ask your accountant to audit charts and financial records.

Taking the time for this now can have a significant impact on your happiness with the deal and in the next several years of your career.

Due Diligence for Sellers

As the seller of a practice, your due diligence tasks begin months or years before deciding to put your practice on the market. If you're thinking about selling, ask yourself the following questions: Am I prepared for outsiders to examine my books and records? Am I comfortable with what they'll find? Am I running personal expenses through the practice? Am I properly classifying my employees and independent contractors? Do I have the required employee policies in place? Do I have a proper lease agreement with adequate renewal periods? These are all things that'll become apparent during a thorough due diligence process.

As a seller, your goal is to get the best possible purchase price for your practice. Any problems revealed during due diligence will likely lower the purchase price. If you do your homework early and get your house in order, your transaction will have a much higher success rate.

As the seller, you want to pay close attention to what the buyer is looking for. Accurately representing your practice from the beginning ensures a better buyer fit. Therefore, even before you go too deeply into the financials, the legal issues, and the contracts, you want to start with this basic question: Is the buyer a match? If you're deeply concerned about your legacy, you'll want to ensure a good cultural fit.

The typical period to prepare for sale is two to three years. Tax returns must be up-to-date and legitimate. Personal expenses, such as vacations and car leases, shouldn't be run through the practice. Spouses and children shouldn't receive employee benefits if they don't work in the business.

You're not only selling a lease, a team, and a reputation; you're also selling your business history. Be sure that you're happy with the kind of story that'll surface when prospective buyers start digging.

Which way is your practice trending? If it's trending downward, you're going to get less money. The best time to sell a practice is when you're adding patients, so as you're preparing your practice for sale, ask yourself whether the trend is positive. Is your business heading in the right direction?

And finally, as a practice owner, are you carrying all the right insurance? This isn't limited to just professional liability insurance. What about employment practices liability insurance? Lots of claims are being made against business owners in today's world. Do you have adequate coverage in place? What about discontinuance of operation coverage and cyber insurance? Most doctors think about malpractice when they think about insurance, but it's a much broader subject. If sexual harassment or wrongful termination claims arise after closing, are you covered?

One Plus One Should Equal Three

In short, you must know what you're buying or what you're selling. It's not how pretty the office is. It's the lease, location, team, practice, reputation, integrity, numbers, trend line for the practice, insurance, and what creditor and lien searches tell us. All of these things affect not only the pricing of the deal but whether the deal should happen at all.

The good news is that if you do your due diligence and really get under the hood of the practice, you can come away with a deal that will benefit you and everyone else involved.

In mergers and acquisitions, attorneys are always looking to see whether one plus one equals three. In other words, if the transaction goes through and everything works out, will the result be greater than the sum of its parts? Will the transaction create so much new value that the deal will be considered a great success by everyone involved? That's what we're looking for: the "one plus one equals three" factor. If that isn't there, it's time to pause and reassess. Don't let anxiety or enthusiasm divert you from getting the information you need and acting appropriately. Don't forget to do your homework.

CHAPTER 3

DRILLING DOWN: WHAT'S A PRACTICE REALLY WORTH?

Everything that can be counted does not necessarily count; everything that counts cannot necessarily be counted.

—William Bruce Cameron

In any marketplace, something is "worth" whatever a buyer is willing to pay and a seller is willing to accept. We refer to this as fair market value. The problem with fair market value is that it doesn't account for intangible factors that are often important to the seller. For example, a practice's worth isn't based on the amount of debt that needs to be paid off. Nor is it based on what the seller thinks she's entitled to in return for building the practice and dedicating many years of her career to the patients and staff. The value of a practice is simply a price on which the buyer and the seller can agree.

In my opinion, a number of market factors have affected how dental practices are valued, and for the most part, these factors have pushed practice prices up. This is great news for sellers, of course, but not necessarily such great news for most buyers. Will the trend last forever? I believe we'll see it continue for the foreseeable future—for the next five years, at least. Beyond that, my crystal ball is cracked. In the meantime, I feel strongly that those who are ready to sell are looking at a fantastic window of opportunity.

When it comes to sale price, think of selling your dental practice in the same way you'd plan to sell your house. Obviously, you want to fetch the highest possible price, but what happens if potential buyers walk in and see that the place hasn't been updated since the 1970s—there's orange shag carpeting on the floor, and the kitchen appliances look like they came from the set of *Little House on the Prairie*? This will, to say the least, have a negative effect on the price.

Does this mean that you should invest a massive sum to update everything in sight? Not necessarily. Most people who've sold homes realize that some remodels and upgrades pay for themselves at selling time, and others don't.

Some strategic spending to ensure your practice looks and feels modern is probably a good idea. But if you're looking to sell in the next couple of years, you probably don't want to invest an excessive amount. The better choice is to keep your eye on the work you're doing and on growing the receipts and profitability, so that you're trending upward when the time comes for buyers to

> **Keep your eye on the work you're doing and on growing the receipts and profitability, so that you're trending upward when the time comes for buyers to look at your numbers.**

look at your numbers. This is probably not the time for major investments, especially ones that won't pay off until after the sale.

Valuation Formulas

Earlier in my career, it seemed as though there was a fairly straightforward formula for determining the value of a dental practice. In that era, the formula was typically between 70 and 80 percent of the average gross receipts for the previous year. We still see this in some transactions, but the analysis has certainly evolved over the years.

As transactions became more sophisticated and dentists became more entrepreneurial, those determining values began incorporating weighted averages into their practice valuations. In this method, we're still looking at 70 to 80 percent of gross receipts, but instead of considering just the current year, we look at the last three fiscal years and weigh them. The current year is weighted the highest, and the most historical is weighted the lowest.

Consider this hypothetical practice: Johnson Dental completed its fiscal year with $1 million in gross revenue. This is an upward trend for the practice, which grossed $900,000 last year and $800,000 two years ago. When Dr. Johnson reaches out to her practice broker to appraise the practice, he suggests they use 75 percent of the three-year weighted average. He explains that these days, sellers are looking to see a more comprehensive valuation, and a three-year weighted average valuation paints a more realistic picture of the practice's value than simply looking at the current year.

To calculate the current fair market value, the broker multiplies the current revenue by three ($1,000,000 × 3), last year's revenue by two ($900,000 × 2), and the prior year's revenue by one ($800,000 × 1). He then adds all three numbers together and divides by six ($5,600,000/6). This results in a weighted average of $933,333, which is then multiplied by 75 percent, for a fair market value of $700,000.

Of course, regardless of the valuation methodology, Johnson Dental's actual selling price will also depend on certain external factors.

Is her practice like the 1970s house we previously discussed, or are the décor and equipment modern and up to date? If the buyer is going to have to spend a lot of money on new equipment and technology, that money is likely to reduce the sale price. Similarly, buyers and lenders weigh the quality and caliber of a practice. Is the practice a very profitable fee-for-service practice, which puts it at the higher end of the value scale, or a good-quality preferred provider organization (PPO) practice, which would be mid- to high-end? A Medicaid practice is often given a lower valuation, even with all other factors being equal.

Sometimes clients ask us whether they should take certain strategic steps to increase their practice's value, such as pursue an acquisition, invest in a practice expansion, develop the ability to do more cosmetic dentistry or implants, increase their marketing budget, and so on. Other practice owners ask us about merging local practices into their locations and bringing in specialists. Are they on the road to building a more valuable practice? In my opinion, yes. However, it all comes down to a cost–benefit analysis. If you're only a year or two away from selling, is it really the time to invest in all these things, or is it better to focus on your top line, keep your expenses lean, and position your practice as a successful business?

This is where the board of directors I described in Chapter 2 comes into play. You want to do this cost–benefit analysis with your team of trusted advisors. This includes your accountant and practice management consultant. They can help you assess what kind of investments you should make. These are decisions no dentist should make without guidance from individuals who understand the marketplace.

Today's Market

Outside of these concerns, two other factors are driving the market up. The first is the availability of 100 percent financing from dental specialty lenders. Dr. Johnson could reasonably say to a potential buyer, "I know that you can get 100 percent of the agreed-on price from the bank in the form of financing. I think that's a fair price." This drives the price higher because, generally speaking, banks consider dentists to be extremely low-risk borrowers. Banks are eager to lend money to dentists looking to buy practices; they know there's a high likelihood the deal will be successful. As dentists have become more entrepreneurial, it's also likely that a dentist who buys one practice may buy others, so banks are looking at the lifetime value of a dentist client and saying, "We can make money with this person (or *from* this person) for years to come, so let's win her first deal and begin building a long-lasting relationship."

DSOs: A Major Factor Driving Prices in the Marketplace

The second factor is the continued expansion of the DSO marketplace and corporate dentistry. Dental service organizations have had a substantial effect on how dental practices are valued. A DSO manages a group of dental practices and may own a portion of the practices' assets. They are often financially backed by private equity groups, but many independent dentists have begun to form their own. This is often referred to as corporate dentistry. The practice of corporate dentistry exists when non-licensed investors, such as private equity groups or other financiers, have equity ownership in certain dental practice assets through the use of a management services company.

In Chapter 7, we'll dive more deeply into the topic of DSOs and whether you should contemplate selling to one or even creating your own. For now, let's consider the effect their existence has on the marketplace in terms of value.

An individual buyer has to be fairly conservative in terms of how much he's going to borrow to buy a practice. After all, the cash flow from that practice is going to provide a living for him and his family, while also providing adequate funding for the practice to grow—and, of course, for the loan to be repaid.

Dental service organizations don't have these types of issues. If Dr. Johnson's practice is the type that attracts DSOs, they recognize they can make money on her practice even if they pay a higher purchase price (possibly 100 percent of the weighted gross receipts, or more, rather than 70 to 80 percent).

An organization with hundreds of millions of dollars can take risks and spend more money than the typical individual whose financial well-being is completely tied to the future of any one practice. Additionally, a DSO can pay more because it has economies of scale that reduce costs in other areas. Lower operating costs offset that up-front cost for the practice itself over time. Therefore, it's not surprising to see dental practices going for higher and higher valuations, because DSOs are reaching higher enterprise values based on the return they can achieve on their investment.

It isn't unheard of for a dentist to receive a letter of intent from a DSO offering more than 100 percent of the practice's gross receipts. These are numbers that were unheard of even a decade ago.

What it comes down to is how DSOs value practices. They use a completely different set of numbers than an independent buyer would. An independent buyer who has graduated from school, then worked as an associate for five years or so, will go to a bank and get a loan when he's ready to buy. The amount he can offer for a practice will be based on servicing that loan while still having enough income to run the practice well and make a living.

Private-equity–backed DSOs, by contrast, look at things differently. They don't care as much about traditional definitions of value. They look at a dental practice's revenue and earnings, and if they can make a 15 percent return on the investment of acquiring a practice then it's a workable deal for them.

So, when a dentist who's been practicing for forty years is getting ready to retire, she may be thinking that she can sell her practice for 70 to 80 percent of her average gross receipts. However, when she gets that letter of intent for 100 percent of gross or more, her view of valuation has skewed upward dramatically. The prices aren't just higher for DSOs making these offers; they are, effectively, higher across the board, whether someone sells to a DSO or not.

There may come a point where this no longer exists, once corporate dentistry saturates the marketplace. Look at the example of today's traditional medical practices: They've been bought up by larger multidiscipline groups or by hospital systems. The doctors no longer own their practices in many cases—they're employees working for salaries. In the world of medical doctors, this model is almost universal today. It's less common to find a completely independent doctor who owns their practice outright and isn't part of a hospital system or a large group practice.

Will corporate dentistry ever reach that sort of marketplace saturation? Probably not, but there will likely come a time when private-equity–backed DSOs will no longer have their checkbooks out the way they do today. If you're considering selling your practice, this may be the perfect time to do so. Between the availability of 100 percent bank financing for buyers and the capital being injected into the market by DSOs, it's a great time to do a deal.

What Dental Practice Buyers Need to Know

Let's look at this era of increasing dental practice valuations from the perspective of the buyer. Assume you're considering purchasing a thirty-year-old practice. The first thing to do is to project its performance over the next ten years. Revenue may drop over the first year or two as some patients leave and as you spend money to update technology, systems, décor, and personnel.

You also must consider locations when you're deciding how much a practice is worth to you. If you know the rents around you have climbed quite a bit but the lease for the office you're looking to buy has a favorable rent with options to renew the existing lease for many years—grab it. A practice in a great location, in a great neighborhood, in a great building, with under-market rent and options to renew, could very well be an opportunity to embrace.

It's important to be conservative in your patient-retention estimates for a general-dentistry practice that accepts reasonable insurance plans. It's probably fair to expect that you'll keep 80 to 85 percent of the patients. Most dentists understand they aren't likely to sustain 100 percent of the current revenue stream immediately on purchase. Project out your revenue, your expenses, and your debt service for the money you'll borrow from the bank to pay for the practice.

When you're valuing a practice, the question becomes this: Once all the expenses are paid, is the practice still profitable? Can you still live your life and pay your bills? Can you pay yourself at least 30 percent of the collectible production for the work you do so that after paying your practice expenses and debt service, you still have some profit? If the answer is yes, then you're looking at a profitable practice.

In my opinion, there are three ways dentists should make money in their practice. First, you should pay yourself like an associate for the dentistry you personally perform (i.e., a percentage of your production). Second, you should pay yourself a salary for serving as the CEO and running the practice (i.e., a management fee). Finally, you should collect net profits from the practice as an equity owner (i.e., distributions).

If the practice isn't profitable enough to pay you for each of these roles (worker, manager, and owner), you may need to take a harder look and be sure that you still see the future upside—or try to negotiate a better price. Purchasing a practice that can only afford to pay you as a working dentist is the equivalent of buying a job. I'd advise someone who brought a deal like this to me for my scrutiny to either negotiate a lower

All too often, dentists think they're buying financial freedom when they're really buying a ten-year job—that is, the amount of time it'll take to pay off the loan.

price or to pass up the deal altogether in favor of a better option.

All too often, dentists think they're buying financial freedom when they're really buying a ten-year job—that is, the amount of time it'll take to pay off the loan. That's why it's essential to work through the future projections in conjunction with your accountant and practice management consultant. It's essential to have a business plan with financial projections to look at the expenses involved in running the practice. What capital improvements are needed? In what years will you be making those capital improvements? If you plan to borrow additional money or lease equipment, you must add those expenses to the budget for each year.

After all of this, will you be making money? If you're barely going to make what you would pay an associate to work in that practice, it's probably not a good deal.

A Bit of Practical Advice

I'm currently representing a seller in a deal that would be fantastic for the buyer if only he could get past his fear of crashing and burning. Maybe he's not getting good professional advice, or perhaps he's scared to take that leap of faith necessary to be a real entrepreneur. The practice is generating more than $2 million a year; it's very profitable. The expenses are in line and typical. The dentist who owns the practice makes a very substantial living. Even the banker called me, because we've worked together on many deals, and said, "I don't know why this guy [the buyer] doesn't get off the dime! After debt service, he's still going to net $300,000 a year in cash profits after paying himself for his productivity and management. What's his problem?"

I bring up this example for two reasons. First, I want to remind you that great deals are out there. It pays to have the patience to find them. Wait, and when you find the right opportunity, jump on it. Make sure your accountant and your advisors agree with you that it's as good as it appears, and then take the leap. You'll be setting yourself and your family up for financial success, and if you don't do it, you'll likely regret it.

The second is a reminder to potential sellers: There are many aspects of your practice that may make it more valuable than you think. If yours is a state-of-the-art practice requiring little to no capital investments, you can likely command top dollar. If you have a growing patient list, that's a valuable asset. If you have a solid, long-term lease, especially in a sought-after neighborhood, that lease will add enormous value to your practice when you're ready to sell.

Anyone can look at today's pricing trends and say, "Dental practices are overpriced. If I'm a seller, I'm going to jump and sell, but if I'm a buyer, I'm going to sit on my hands." In reality, there's a premium you have to pay for anything in life that's worthwhile, whether it's a beautiful house, a fancy car, or even a great bottle of wine. Accepting the higher cost means potentially winning a greater reward.

Keep in mind what I've shared with you about valuations in this chapter. Obviously, if a deal seems too good to be true, we all know what that means. But there really are a lot of great deals out there. Even if you have to pay a little more than you expected to get a great practice, you'll ultimately make the money back. Sitting on your hands or buying a less expensive practice that turns into that dreaded ten-year job—that's not the way to go.

Understand the value of the practices that you're considering buying, find the one that makes the most sense, and then make the move. Remember, you aren't only a practitioner; you're an entrepreneur.

A Final Note

It's important to remember that a deal is more than just numbers. Not long ago, someone came to me and told me that a particular dentist had been so deeply affected by issues in his personal life that his practice was suffering financially and could be purchased at a "fire sale" price. I stayed away because I don't like to get involved in situations where there are winners and losers. If everybody doesn't feel the deal was mutually beneficial and successful for both sides, then the transaction isn't something I want any part of. I hope that whoever represents you feels the same way.

CHAPTER 4

LET'S MAKE A DEAL: UNDERSTANDING THE FINANCIAL TERMS

Money isn't the most important thing in life, but it's reasonably close to oxygen on the "gotta have it" scale.

—Zig Ziglar

Regarding the money part of any deal, there are three equally important components: How much is being paid? Where is the money coming from? And when does the seller get it? In the last chapter, we focused on the "how much." In this chapter, we'll focus on the "where" and "when."

Cash Deals and Seller Financing

Banks love dentists, as I've pointed out, because they have a great risk profile. The default rate among dentists is said to be no more than 1 percent nationwide. Banks have responded to this statistic by creating specialty lending groups focused solely on health care and even more narrowly focused on the purchase of dental practices. If you're a buyer, the good news is you're likely to get all the money you need. If you're the seller in an outright sale (known as a "cash deal"), you're going to get all of your money at the time of closing. This is a great option for dentists who wish to retire immediately to spend their days golfing in Florida or Arizona.

There are concerns to note, however, if you're the buyer. Let's say the practice isn't everything that the seller represented it to be, and you have to go after that seller in a post-closing dispute. Now, the seller has the full purchase price in her pocket, and you, the buyer, have to spend money on lawyers to get the whole thing straightened out. In the earlier days of my career, more deals were seller financed (meaning, the seller lent the buyer the money rather than the bank doing so). As a result, sellers were highly incentivized to facilitate a practice's post-closing success because they didn't get all the money up front; payouts typically took years. Today's changing realities mean that buyers must be more cautious.

If you're the buyer and things don't proceed as expected, keep in mind that a bank isn't going to patiently wait for you to straighten things out with the seller. The lender will expect you to continue the terms of the loan agreement. This is why your due diligence is so important in the first stage of the sale. When you've done your homework, a cash deal should be uncomplicated and fast for both the buyer and the seller.

When you've done your homework, a cash deal should be uncomplicated and fast for both the buyer and the seller.

From a bank's perspective, the most desirable deal involves a solid general-dentistry practice that takes quality insurance plans. These types of practices have a steady flow of income, patients typically stay with the practice, and the dentist isn't dependent on referrals from other doctors. Typically, life goes on as usual after the sale, especially if the staff and location remain the same.

Acquiring specialty practices involves a little more risk because they depend on referrals from general dentists to generate patients. In those cases, valuations may be lower, but a bank may not be willing to lend 100 percent of the purchase price, and it may want the seller to hold a promissory note for the difference. This is actually a positive in my view when representing a buyer, because the seller now has a stake in the game in the form of a vested interest in the buyer's post-closing success. In such cases, the seller is more likely to make herself available to the buyer during the transition period to make sure everything goes smoothly.

It's less common today, but in some cases, the seller of a practice will request seller financing. In these cases, the seller may say, "I'd like to hold the note myself because that way I won't have to pay all the taxes on the deal in the first year." In this scenario, the payments are spread out, and the seller doesn't have to report all of the gain on the sale in a single year. This type of arrangement is known as an "installment sale," and a seller who can wait for the full proceeds of a sale may find that this is advantageous for tax purposes.

Next, let's consider a transaction in which an associate or an outsider is buying into a portion of a practice, rather than buying the entire practice. In these cases, the lender typically requires a corporate guarantee from the practice. That way, if the buyer ever defaults on the loan, the bank can pursue payment from the practice itself or go after its assets. Some dentists who are selling a minority interest in their practice are comfortable with this approach because they're confident in their relationship with the associate buyer and confident in the practice's historical performance. Others don't like it because they believe they're essentially guaranteeing their transaction; if the buyer defaults, the selling dentist is on the hook to finance her purchase price.

In some cases, instead of signing a corporate guarantee, the seller opts to hold the note instead of having the bank hold it. If all goes well, the seller will earn interest as she collects the principal. In the case of a default, the seller can simply take back the minority interest that she sold and keep the payments she's received thus far.

Earn-outs

An earn-out deal is a transaction in which the buyer of a practice pays the seller a percentage of the practice's gross receipts for a specified period. Most often we see a payment term of five years, but this can vary depending on the value of the practice and the other deal terms. As the practice grows, the buyer makes installment payments to the seller based on the performance of the practice after the closing.

The first time I saw the earn-out strategy applied in the context of a dental practice transaction was with clients of Fortune Practice Management. The strategy is well documented in a book written by Bernie Stoltz and Mark Murphy, titled *The Win-Win Outcome: The Dealmaker's Guide to Buying and Selling Dental Practices.* In these instances, everyone wins: The seller is happy because she is potentially paid more than she would've gotten in a cash deal, and the buyer is happy because he didn't assume any risk by taking on a loan.

Earn-outs also can be highly advantageous because they offer a great incentive to build the business. A buyer has the freedom to invest time, energy, and money to grow the practice because he isn't saddled with a loan. Instead, his payments are equal to a percentage of gross receipts, often ranging from 10 to 20 percent. If his payments rise, it's because the practice's earnings grew.

A seller remains invested in the practice's success because her final selling price is directly linked to it. If she stays and helps the new owner succeed, she succeeds too. A well-structured earn-out is a winning scenario for all involved.

I could get granular and describe all sorts of specific scenarios that might make fascinating reading if you, too, happen to be an attorney who works with dentists on sales and acquisitions. But suffice it to say that there's no one right way to construct a deal. There are often innovative options for structuring a sale that can make the deal more advantageous to both buyer and seller. If you have a sophisticated attorney on your side, you may be able to come up with a creative approach that will put more money into the pockets of both sides while reducing the risks for all involved.

Associate Discount Programs

A "sweat equity" discount program may be appropriate when a junior associate comes on board and isn't quite ready to buy into the practice. In some cases, the senior dentist running the practice wants to give the young associate some time to prove himself but also wants to incentivize the associate to help grow the practice and eventually become a minority partner.

A great way to do this is to offer the associate a discount on his future buy-in, the amount of which is directly linked to his current performance. In this scenario, the practice agrees to calculate an amount each month equal to a percentage (typically 2–5 percent) of the associate's overall gross collections. We refer to this as the sweat equity discount. This discount accumulates each month, and when the time comes for the associate to buy an interest in the practice, the purchase price for that interest (equal to the fair market value of the interest at the time of closing) will be reduced by the amount of the sweat equity discount.

This incentivizes the younger dentist to perform at a higher level, because the more his collections are, the more money will go into the sweat equity discount and lower his future purchase price will be.

In this case, you aren't using actual money to do this, and that's something that dentists greatly appreciate. You're essentially creating a discount program for the associate. This is a great way to create some loyalty and incentivize the younger dentist to not only do a great job but also to stay with the practice; he will get a piece of the pie in the form of a future discount.

This type of planning essentially creates junior golden handcuffs by connecting the young dentist to the practice in a meaningful way. Instead of looking around to see what else is out there, he remains loyal to the practice, helps to grow the patient base, and eventually benefits from the sweat equity discount that's been accruing on his behalf.

Everybody wins because the practice grows, turnover is reduced, and the young dentist feels as though he has a stake in the outcome rather than only a salary. When deals are structured well, everyone is happy.

These types of arrangements have tax implications, so you want to make sure that your attorney and accountant are well versed in these matters. Having all of your experts work together means creating a deal that results in success for all parties.

DSO Payment Terms

We'll discuss selling to DSOs in greater detail in Chapter 7, but since we're on the topic of financial deal terms, it's worth touching briefly on typical DSO sale structures. When you're selling to DSOs, they tend to pay a fairly large portion of the purchase price in cash at the closing. But they'll often try to protect themselves, either by having the seller hold a promissory note for a portion of the price or by insisting on an earn-out portion with incentive payments based on the future performance of the practice.

Private equity groups also typically structure their deals with what we call *rollover equity*. They often pay 70 to 80 percent in cash at the time of closing, and the remainder in the form of stock or equity in the DSO itself.

DSOs typically look for long-term employment agreements, often requiring the selling dentist to stay with the practice for a minimum of three to five years after the closing. This provides the DSO a degree of continuity from the seller's management era to theirs. DSOs don't want to invest time immediately after a transaction trying to find new associates. They prefer to leave day-to-day operations in the hands of the people most familiar with the practice, the staff, the patients, and so forth.

Dental service organizations are looking to maintain or increase cash flow, return on their investment, and continue operating the practice in the ordinary course of business. They'll lower overhead through streamlining of functions, adherence to their standardized business practices, and economies of scale.

Dental service organizations use rollover equity to incentivize the seller to maximize the success of the brand and the practice after the closing and thus increase the value of her remaining ownership interest. Over time, the seller may go out and find other target acquisitions, because she now has stock in the company. In other words, the DSO is actually enrolling the selling dentist as a referral source for more deals. Because the selling dentist now has a piece of the action, in terms of equity in the DSO, it's in her best interest to grow the business and go out and find great deals for the DSO. After all, who knows the local market better than a respected local dentist?

CHAPTER 5

NAVIGATING THE TRANSITION PERIOD

*Change is the law of life and those who look only to the
past or present are certain to miss the future.*

—John F. Kennedy

Here's the great news: The process of conducting due diligence and negotiating the terms of the financial deal is the hardest and most time-consuming part of a dental practice transaction. If you've made it this far, congratulations! You're well on your way to a successful closing.

The next step in the process is to negotiate and draft the transaction documents. This requires a deep dive into the details of how the practice will transition from the seller to the buyer. Our goal, as transactional attorneys, is to make sure that the legal documents cover every aspect of this transition so there's no room for any misunderstanding or argument after the closing.

In this chapter, we'll address the length of the transition period and what you may expect during that time. We'll also talk about what you can do to make this period smooth and productive.

Let's look at some different situations to see how the transition period can vary. For the sake of simplicity, we'll call the selling dentist "Dr. Sally" and the buying dentist "Dr. Bill."

Our dentists are engaged in an outright cash purchase of a general dentistry practice whose business is mostly insurance-based. After the closing, Dr. Bill intends to keep Dr. Sally's current practice location, retain all her staff members, and continue to accept all the same insurance plans. Given these facts, we can expect that most of Dr. Sally's patients will stay with the practice even after Dr. Bill becomes the owner. Dr. Bill should get at least one chance to prove himself to Dr. Sally's patients.

Dr. Sally is eager to retire. She plans to move closer to her grandkids. However, the sale of a dental practice isn't a transaction in which you leave the keys on the counter on your way out the door. Dr. Sally wants her successor to succeed. She also wants to preserve her legacy. The best way for Dr. Sally to ensure the practice's future success is to assist Dr. Bill for a reasonable period after the closing.

First, the patients will need to establish a comfortable rapport with their new doctor. Most patients at a practice like this are willing to give the new dentist an opportunity to prove that he's a decent person and a competent dentist; we call this *one bite at the apple.*

In this scenario—involving a general dentistry practice that accepts most insurance plans—a reasonable transition period would be six to twelve months. The goal should be to get through at least one hygiene cycle with most active patients. Most patients come in twice a year for a cleaning and an examination, so over a six-month period, the new dentist will see most of the practice's patients. By giving it a full year, Dr. Bill can be sure he's seen all the patients, even those treated outside their normal schedule.

During the transition period, Dr. Sally will facilitate introductions among Dr. Bill, the staff, the vendors, and any referral sources. This gives these key players adequate time to adjust to Dr. Bill and the way he likes to operate his office. During this period, Dr. Sally will also handle any corrective treatment issues that arise as a result of work that she performed before the closing.

There are many ways to structure a short transition period. For instance, Dr. Sally may agree to work her regular schedule for six months, as if she were an associate working for Dr. Bill. Then Dr. Sally may agree to work part-time for an additional three months and then be available for phone consultations for the last three months.

However anxious Dr. Sally is to get on with the next phase of her life, her investment in this transition period will be crucial to Dr. Bill's success.

Next, let's assess how the transition period might differ in a fee-for-service general dentistry practice that doesn't take any insurance. Dr. Sally's patients have happily paid her fees for years because they like seeing her. These patients have the resources to go anywhere they want for their dental work; their choices aren't limited by insurance plans. In a situation like this, it's critical for Dr. Sally to introduce Dr. Bill to each of the patients individually. Without Dr. Sally's full endorsement, these high-end patients may not be as likely to give Dr. Bill a chance.

In this scenario, we'd recommend a transition period of at least one year or possibly longer. Because a personal introduction with each patient is essential, this will likely take longer than the standard six months. Often in these cases, the selling dentist will agree to stay on chairside for at least a year, initially maintaining her normal schedule, and then decreasing hours incrementally each quarter. At the end of the first year, the selling doctor will often agree to make herself available as a consultant on an as-needed basis for an additional six months to a year. The more time she spends in that role, the better off she is for the long-term health of the practice she has dedicated years to developing.

The third transition scenario I'd like to discuss is the specialty practice. This is a different animal entirely from a general dentistry practice, whether it's an insurance-oriented practice or a fee-for-service practice. In a specialty practice, you're transferring not only the patients but also the referral relationships. Dr. Bill will need to develop relationships with the referring dentists who've been sending patients to Dr. Sally for all these years. You never want to assume that a referral source will turn over patients to an unproven Dr. Bill after all those successful years with Dr. Sally, even on Dr. Sally's recommendation. It takes a smooth, well-considered transition to make it work.

The ideal scenario is one in which Dr. Bill first becomes an associate or a junior partner in the practice, working for Dr. Sally for at least a couple of years. With this approach, Dr. Bill gets to know the staff, the patients, and the referral sources well. As he earns their trust, he becomes the logical successor for the practice.

When buying or selling a specialty practice, keep in mind that a longer transition process helps to ensure that the buyer maintains the same successful relationships with the referral sources that the seller has always enjoyed.

Whether the practice is insurance-based, fee-for-service, or a specialty, communication from the selling doctor to patients and referral sources is vitally important. Dr. Sally should assure her patients—ideally in writing—that Dr. Bill shares her values. Dr. Sally should communicate to them that the staff is going to remain, so it's still the same practice they've always loved. "The dental hygienists aren't going anywhere, so you can count on that friendly face, the person who remembers details, like your kids' names, from one hygiene appointment to the next." Dr. Sally should also remind patients that their records will stay in the same place; the transition will be smooth.

Finally, Dr. Sally should invite her patients to come in and meet Dr. Bill so they can begin to develop a relationship with him. This sets the practice up to succeed after the sale has closed.

These are all things that can ensure a smooth transition. Unfortunately, there are also many factors that make a transition harder or even threaten its success. For example, it's not unheard of for a selling doctor to sabotage the buyer as the result of her ego.

In most cases, the selling doctor is going to stay on for two or three days a week, working as an associate, making introductions, or helping out with the transition. If you're the buyer, you have to be protected in the event that the relationship sours. If Dr. Sally starts bad-mouthing Dr. Bill to the patients, undermining his treatment plans, or otherwise allowing her ego to interfere with the transition, things aren't going to end well. As the new dentist, Dr. Bill only gets one bite of the apple; if patients aren't comfortable, they're going to take their business somewhere else.

Dr. Bill will have a real problem on his hands if his post-closing employment agreement with Dr. Sally only allows him to terminate her with "cause." Generally speaking, personality conflicts aren't grounds for terminating an employee with cause. A safer agreement will specify that Dr. Bill can terminate Dr. Sally's employment for any reason during the transition period, not just for cause. Otherwise, the purchaser could be stuck with an unworkable relationship. If Dr. Bill fires Dr. Sally before her employment agreement ends, he runs the risk of Dr. Sally filing a lawsuit against him for breach of contract. This is the kind of serious issue that needs to be resolved in advance of the closing so as to minimize problems down the road.

Corrective Treatment after Closing

Any well-drafted purchase agreement will include a comprehensive corrective treatment provision. This is essentially the seller's warranty of the dental treatment provided to patients before the closing. During the transition period, the seller will guarantee her work. If any patient presents with a problem during the transition period, the seller agrees to either perform the corrective treatment herself or reimburse the buyer for his expense in performing such corrective treatment.

Assume that a crown is set in a patient's mouth before the closing and it fails four weeks after the closing. Who is responsible for repairing or replacing the crown? Without a corrective treatment provision, the seller has no liability for the cost of the repair, and it'll be up to the buyer to either fix the problem or lose the patient.

A typical corrective treatment provision offers a six- to twelve-month warranty on all dental treatment performed before closing. Assuming that Dr. Sally has agreed to stay at the practice as an employee during the transition period, the agreement will likely permit her to perform the corrective treatment using the practice's staff. If Dr. Sally is unavailable or refuses to honor the warranty, Dr. Bill will have the right to treat the patient and bill Dr. Sally for his costs.

The corrective treatment provision should also address issues such as when corrective treatment is necessary and what happens when the doctors don't agree. For instance, Dr. Sally may review a patient chart and determine that corrective treatment isn't warranted in a particular case and, therefore, refuse to warranty her work. In one extreme case we handled, the buyer of a practice didn't like any of the work that the seller had done and started redoing absolutely everything on practically every patient. The seller was outraged. She told the buyer, "I've never had anyone come back for corrective treatment; you're actually creating these problems yourself!" Fortunately, there was an arbitration clause built into that agreement, so they were able to resolve the matter without going to court.

Typically, state dental associations also have alternative dispute mechanisms to help unhappy doctors avoid litigation. It's best to have those mechanisms specified in the purchase agreement, because clear agreements help avoid future conflicts.

In another transaction we handled, the buyer purchased a dental practice riddled with problems. There were substantial defects in the dentistry. It wasn't only that the work was subpar; patients were actually injured by the selling dentist. This forced the buyer to make some tough choices. The economics were brutal, as he'd already invested more than $1 million in the practice.

Before the closing, the buyer spent little time chairside; he was very entrepreneurial and had purchased numerous practices, installing associates in each. He expected to do the same thing with this practice. Instead, he realized this was a crisis, and he needed to take care of the patients and make sure they all had healthy mouths. So, he rolled up his sleeves, and for three days a week over the course of six months, he worked on every patient until he had fixed every problem. Of course, he would've preferred to spend that time finding and buying new practices, but he had to do the dental work himself to save his investment in the practice. The matter ultimately ended up in litigation.

Once again, this brings us back to the importance of due diligence. If the buyer had checked with the state board before the purchase, he would've found many complaints and disciplinary actions taken against the selling dentist. He also should've interviewed the staff before the closing and asked how often patients came in for corrective treatment.

While avoiding the purchase altogether might have been the best course of action, a good purchase agreement that protected the doctor during the transition would've been the second line of defense. Unfortunately, we weren't hired until after the damage was done and the contracts were signed.

> **Most transitions are smooth, and all parties are generally happy with the result. But preparation is key.**

The good news is that these cases are rare. Most transitions are smooth, and all parties are generally happy with the result. But preparation is key. When you spell out what everyone should expect, you have a better chance of a transition that will meet those expectations.

Work in Progress

Work in progress is another critically important issue that must be dealt with in the purchase agreement. It's all but impossible to time a closing date for the sale of a dental practice when there are zero cases in progress. Many procedures that dentists perform require a multistep treatment plan; for example, you might have prepped a crown but haven't cemented it yet.

The work-in-progress section of your purchase agreement should address the following: What percentage of the work was done before the closing, what services need to be provided after closing, who will complete the treatment plan, who will keep the amounts paid before closing, and who will keep the amounts paid after closing? In addition, if the selling dentist is doing the work, the agreement should state how much time she'll have to complete the work in progress, whether she'll be permitted to use the buyer's office location and staff, whether she'll be required to pay for using the office equipment and staff, and who'll pay for out-of-pocket costs.

One scenario that's often missed when discussing work in progress is the issue of post-closing employment. As we've discussed, it's very common for a selling dentist to continue working at the practice for a period after the closing. Typically, the seller will be compensated for her services based on a percentage of collections. However, this raises the question as to whether the selling dentist should be compensated for collections received for the completion of work in progress. Generally, this depends on the percentage of the work completed and the percentage of payment collected before the closing.

Needless to say, it's imperative that all parties fully understand the expectations surrounding work in progress before the close of the transaction.

Reasonable Restrictive Covenants

Simply stated, a restrictive covenant is a limitation on the seller's conduct after the closing. Typically, four restrictive covenants apply in dental practice transactions: confidentiality, non-disparagement, non-competition, and non-solicitation.

Confidentiality is a concept that dentists understand well. When you sell a practice, not only do you remain bound by the Health Insurance Portability and Accountability Act (HIPAA) and other laws governing patient confidentiality, you also promise not to disclose confidential information related to the business itself. This includes items such as the patient list, financial records, employee information, billing practices, marketing strategies, referral sources, supplier lists, and any other business information that is unique or proprietary to the practice.

A non-disparagement covenant is a promise not to make any offensive, insulting, or harmful statements about the other party or the quality of the services he or she rendered, even when such statements may be true. These provisions can be unilateral or mutual. Generally speaking, a purchase agreement will state that the seller can't disparage the buyer or the practice. This is known as a *unilateral* clause because only one party is restricted. However, if Dr. Sally is concerned about preserving her image and reputation after the closing, she may request that the provision be made *mutual*. In other words, that Dr. Bill also be barred from making any negative statements about her after the closing. This is a very common and reasonable request, but as the seller, if you don't request it, it typically won't be offered to you.

Non-competition and non-solicitation clauses are standard in every dental practice transaction. The non-compete provision is a prohibition on practicing dentistry or owning a competing dental practice within a specified territory for a specified period. A non-solicitation provision, on the other hand, prevents the selling dentist from soliciting patients, employees, and often referral sources of the practice after the closing.

Unfortunately, every state has its own take on the enforceability of non-competition agreements. However, if properly written, in the context of a business sale, they're permissible. As a rule, for a non-compete to be enforceable, it must be "reasonable" in both its time and geography. The definitions of "reasonable" vary wildly and depend entirely on the location and the local market.

For example, in rural Texas, it may be reasonable to dictate that a seller won't practice dentistry within a twenty-mile radius of the office. That same restricted radius would be completely unreasonable in any major city. Restrictions in New York City, for example, must be stated in terms of several blocks surrounding the office, because a few miles would wipe out most of Manhattan. In short, the restriction must be "reasonable" for a court to enforce it and for it to be agreeable to both buyer and seller.

In most cases, non-competition periods range from three to five years post-closing. Non-solicitation periods, on the other hand, range from one to five years post-closing.

It's also important to note that many states are reluctant to enforce non-competition agreements in employment agreements, and some states even have a complete ban on restricting employees from competing. However, almost every state permits non-competes in the context of selling a business. This is because the seller of a business (as opposed to an employee) is receiving substantial consideration (in the form of the purchase price) for her promise not to compete. As such, she's expected, as part of that deal, to transfer the goodwill of the business to the buyer. If Dr. Sally immediately sets up shop not far from where Dr. Bill has taken over her practice, she'll diminish the value of the practice after the closing date. Purchase agreements should ensure that this doesn't happen, and so long as the terms are reasonable, courts will enforce them.

Lenders also have strong opinions about covenants not to compete. If Dr. Bill doesn't get at least a three- or four-year non-competition clause in the purchase agreement, most banks won't lend him the money to buy the practice. They know that if Dr. Sally competes with Dr. Bill for the same patients, the practice could collapse, the buyer will default, and the loan will go bad.

Let's turn briefly to the subject of non-solicitation clauses. Typically, the boilerplate language in a purchase agreement doesn't specify what "solicitation" means. This leaves open the possibility of a situation in which Dr. Sally continues to see some of Dr. Bill's patients. Without the proper language, Dr. Bill is going to have a hard time proving that Dr. Sally reached out to the patient first, instead of the other way around.

That's why I insist on much more powerful language for the non-solicitation clause. The agreements our firm creates for our clients who are buying practices state, "The seller shall not *perform services* for the patient." This removes any uncertainty about what the seller's obligations are to the buyer. It's no longer a question of who contacted whom; Dr. Sally isn't allowed to perform any services for patients of her old practice, period. I highly recommend that language, and the only way to ensure that it's correctly written is to have an agreement crafted by a knowledgeable attorney.

Employees versus Independent Contractors

One of the most common issues we see in dental practice transactions is the misclassification of dentists as independent contractors. This is a frequent topic of discussion in cases in which the selling dentist intends to continue treating patients after the closing. Will the buyer engage the seller as an employee or as an independent contractor?

Although buyers and sellers may both have good tax reasons for wanting to treat the selling dentist as an independent contractor, the IRS has very strict guidelines about who may and may not be classified as an independent contractor. In addition, many states have adopted even stricter guidelines for classifying independent contractors.

This classification analysis is very state-specific and must be analyzed on a case-by-case basis. However, misclassifying an employee as an independent contractor can be very costly. States audit businesses, searching for these misclassifications. If they determine that an individual should have been treated as an employee, the practice can be held liable for unpaid payroll taxes and unpaid unemployment insurance tax, along with penalties and interest for failure to comply with withholding requirements.

Employment taxes and penalties are huge money-makers for state governments. They love to audit small businesses. They're reluctant to negotiate penalties, particularly when it's clear the practice exercised complete control over the dentist's workload and schedule, or the dentist didn't work anywhere else.

As a business owner, it's important to understand your state's employment laws if you're considering selling your practice.

Managing the Moving Parts

The transition process may seem difficult or even impossible to manage with so many moving parts, and, of course, the issues we've talked about in this chapter must be dealt with before closing. But if those issues are faced head-on and handled properly, Dr. Bill will end up with a successful practice, and Dr. Sally can sail off into the sunset (after her transition period ends), secure in the knowledge that her patients and team are well taken care of.

CHAPTER 6

THE PROS AND CONS OF BUYING IN

Opportunities come infrequently. When it rains gold,
put out the bucket, not the thimble.

—Warren Buffett

Throughout this book, we've focused primarily on dental practice transactions involving the complete transfer of a practice from one owner to the next. Dental practice transactions often involve the sale of only a fraction of the practice (typically a minority interest) to an associate employee. These minority interest transactions, or buy-ins, can be extremely advantageous to both the seller and the buyer.

From the perspective of the senior dentist, an associate buy-in is a great succession plan. Now, instead of just being an employee, the junior dentist is an owner, which makes it much more likely that he'll remain loyal to the practice, work hard to grow the practice, and generally act and think like someone who has a valuable stake in its future.

This process also allows a senior dentist to handpick a successor rather than selling the practice to a stranger. An associate who buys into a practice has already proven to the owner, the team, and the patients that he's capable, competent, and a good fit.

Bringing on a partner also creates a bit of an insurance policy in that the agreements governing the partnership generally mandate that in the event of a partner's death, disability, or retirement, the remaining partner must buy out the deceased, disabled, or retired partner's interest for fair market value. Without a partner, the death of a practice owner could mean the death of the practice, with no money passing to the owner's family.

From the perspective of the associate, a buy-in can be an amazing business opportunity. The associate gets to share in the upside of the practice instead of simply collecting a salary. In addition, a buy-in allows the associate to "dip a toe in the water" as an entrepreneur without taking the full risk that comes with owning 100 percent of a practice. While a minority owner, the junior dentist will have the opportunity to learn from the senior dentist all that's required to run and manage a profitable dental practice effectively. When successful, the education that comes from an associate buy-in can be an advantage over an outright purchase.

In this chapter, we're going to talk about the pros and cons of bringing in an associate, how to do it the right way, what the pitfalls are, and how to avoid those pitfalls so that the transition from associate to partner is as smooth as possible.

More Than Just a Business Decision

The first issue to address is culture. In a traditional practice sale, where complete ownership is transferred, the buyer and seller are forced to play a very quick—and not always successful—game of "getting to know you." Who is this other person? Will the buyer fit within the practice's culture? Is the buyer happy with the office location? Is there cultural and philosophical alignment between the two dentists? This isn't only a business decision; selling a practice can be a very emotional experience. If you've been practicing dentistry for decades, your practice may very well be your identity. In many cases, what you do as a dentist is who you *are* as a person.

> If you've been practicing dentistry for decades, your practice may very well be your identity.

That's not true for every dentist, of course. We've had some clients who were hitting golf balls in Florida sixty days after selling their practices. For most dentists, however, practicing dentistry has become part of their DNA and a huge part of their identity. They love their work, they love their patients and staff, and their practice is part of their legacy to the world . . . so it can be unsettling for them to sell it to a stranger.

This is why selling a minority interest in your practice to an associate and making an arrangement for that associate to one day buy the entire practice is often the smoothest way to create a transition for all involved. Selling 100 percent of your practice to a stranger can be very jarring for the team and the patients. Selling a piece of the practice to an associate avoids that abrupt change and makes for a smoother, more gradual transition.

We usually recommend that senior dentists start by selling the associate a small minority interest in the practice rather than an equal 50 percent share (I'm not a fan of fifty/fifty deals). When the senior dentist sells a minority interest, she's still in total control of the business and maintains all the decision-making authority. In my experience, it's best for the practice to have one ultimate boss.

The Buy-in Timeline

Associate buy-ins generally take place in two steps. The associate purchases an initial minority interest in the practice. We'll talk about the dangers of a fifty/fifty ownership later in this chapter, but for now, let's just say that the ideal starting point is typically 10 to 20 percent of the practice. This allows for a testing period to make sure that the associate really lives up to his part of the bargain. It's a lot easier to unwind a transaction involving 10 to 20 percent of a practice than 50 percent—or the whole thing.

The second step is a complete buyout of the senior dentist's remaining interest in the practice. The second step will typically take place on the occurrence of a future triggering event, such as the senior dentist's death, disability, or retirement.

Once the associate purchases an initial ownership interest, the tendency is for everyone involved to take him more seriously. He'll have an opportunity to develop a deeper relationship with the staff and referral sources, and he should have their complete confidence when he eventually buys out the entire practice. When things happen this way, the transition is practically seamless because the buyer has already been a partner with an ownership share, and he's worked there for a meaningful amount of time. As a result, the associate dentist's contribution is much greater than it would've been had he remained on salary without an ownership stake.

This raises the important question of how to value the associate's contribution during the period between his initial purchase and the subsequent buyout of the remaining interest in the practice.

The selling dentist may say, "I'm expecting a new valuation on the practice because I ought to be rewarded for the entrepreneurial risk of hiring you and selling you a percentage." The associate will likely respond, "I believe I'm the one who should be rewarded. I helped contribute to the growth of the practice with my skills, my management abilities, and everything I've done for the practice. Since I helped the practice grow, aren't you effectively making me pay more for something I helped create?"

These are both valid points. The senior dentist did take a risk by hiring the associate and should be rewarded for taking that risk. At the same time, the associate's contributions to the growth of the practice should be recognized and rewarded.

The way to settle this argument—which happens more often than you might think—is to start off by recognizing that both points of view are valid. The associate did contribute to the increased value of the practice, and the senior dentist did assume the bulk of the risk.

We suggest looking at the difference between the initial valuation of the practice when the associate first bought in and the current value of the practice. We often recommend a compromise that provides the seller a portion of the upside—not all of it, but maybe 50 to 75 percent—while also including a "floor" price of no less than the original value of the practice at the time of the initial buy-in. This approach, or something similar, is often acceptable to both parties as a fair compromise.

Consider this example: A dental practice is worth $1 million today, and Dr. Simon has agreed to sell Dr. Alex a 10 percent interest. Dr. Alex takes out a loan and pays Dr. Simon $100,000 for his interest. On the closing date, Dr. Simon and Dr. Alex enter into a partnership agreement to govern the future ownership and management of the practice. The partnership agreement states that once Dr. Simon turns sixty-five, he'll have the right to retire, at which time Dr. Alex will be required to purchase Dr. Simon's remaining 90 percent interest in the practice.

Dr. Alex and Dr. Simon successfully negotiated a formula for valuing Dr. Simon's 90 percent interest in the practice, which is contained in the partnership agreement. It states that in the event of Dr. Simon's retirement, Dr. Alex will pay Dr. Simon an amount equal to the fair market value of Dr. Simon's 90 percent interest in the practice as of the date of retirement, less a 30 percent discount. Assuming that the fair market value when Dr. Simon retires is $2 million, the purchase price will be $1,260,000, which is calculated as follows:

$2,000,000 × 0.9 = $1,800,000 = fair market value of 90 percent interest

$1,800,000 × 0.7 = $1,260,000 = purchase price minus 30 percent discount

The Benefits of Selling to an Associate

In a traditional sale to an outside buyer, the transfer of goodwill is a primary concern. As we discussed, a solid cultural fit is required to successfully transfer relationships with patients, referral sources, and staff members. When an associate buys in, very little transition is required.

In situations such as this, there's an automatic transfer of goodwill from the senior dentist to the associate because the associate has an existing relationship with these individuals.

Selling a piece of a practice is also a wise move for the entrepreneurial dentist who owns multiple practices and has hired associates to run each of them. When I work with multi-practice operators, I often recommend they sell a minority piece of each practice to associates who've proven themselves to be competent, hardworking, entrepreneurial, and committed to the growth of that practice.

When you sell a minority interest to an associate, you're creating "stickiness." The associate is more likely to stick around and grow that practice instead of looking at potentially greener pastures somewhere else.

Also, a multi-practice operator can't be everywhere all the time. If you own three or more practices, it might make sense to consider allowing a junior associate to invest in a portion of each practice. The associate gets to be a practice owner, and you get a loyal partner to help manage and grow your location.

Everyone in the industry talks about the difficulty of retaining great associates. Associates with an equity interest are able to make more money, have a stake in the practice's future, and ultimately are going to help you scale.

Not all dentists want to sit chairside with a handpiece after a certain point in their career. Some prefer instead to be "CEO dentists" who own and operate multiple practices. The benefits are manifold: your bottom-line increases, your retention increases, and the operating dentist, the team, and the patients are all happier. Everybody wins.

In this sense, the entrepreneurial senior dentist is operating like a mini-DSO. Allowing associates to own minority interests in each practice is what makes it possible to operate in this way.

Accounting for Risk

The shift in power from the senior dentist to the junior associate isn't the only potential issue that needs to be considered when selling a minority interest in a practice. If the junior associate needs bank financing to pay the purchase price, the bank will often require that the practice itself provide a corporate guarantee of the junior associate's loan. This means the senior dentist is taking a risk if, for any reason, the associate is unable to repay the loan.

In these situations, the seller should be compensated for that risk. This is often accounted for when negotiating other aspects of the partnership agreement. For example, the senior dentist may argue that the junior associate should have very limited voting power over day-to-day management issues. Alternatively, the senior dentist may use this as leverage to negotiate more favorable buy–sell terms.

One final risk consideration for sellers is the sharing of control. Once you bring on a partner, the partnership and the laws governing your corporate entity will give your junior partner certain rights with respect to management and decision-making. Regardless of what your partnership agreement might say, certain rights are granted as a matter of law, and you can't always "contract around them." This is an issue you'll want to discuss with your attorney before signing the partnership agreement.

The Benefits of Buying In

So far, we've been talking about the benefits of selling a piece of the practice primarily from the perspective of the seller. But we don't always represent the seller; quite often we represent the associate who's buying in. Let's take a moment now to talk about the benefits to the associate buyer.

First, becoming an entrepreneur requires a willingness to take on certain calculated risks. The best way to minimize risk as a young, entrepreneurial dentist is to go to work for a practice, and as soon as you verify that it's a good fit and a high-quality practice, try to explore your options for a future buy-in.

Although the typical due diligence period on the purchase of an entire dental practice may be several weeks or months, an associate's due diligence begins on the first day he or she steps foot in the office. In most cases, this means that the associate potentially has years to assess the practice before actually buying a minority interest. No outside buyer could ever know that practice better than the associate because the associate has worked closely with the team members and understands and contributes to the office's culture. You've seen behind the curtain, as it were, and due diligence doesn't get any better than that.

So, buying into a well-established practice where you've worked for a meaningful period is often the best-case scenario for a young dentist who aspires to be an owner. After all, if you've been there for a few years, you're in the best position to know whether it's a good fit from a cultural and philosophical standpoint, and therefore, whether you should buy in.

Cultivating a Productive Relationship

Once money changes hands and the associate owns a piece of the practice, the relationship between the senior dentist and the junior partner needs to change both publicly and on paper. It's essential that the senior dentist avoid treating the junior partner as an employee. We've talked already about the need for the senior dentist to check his or her ego at the door, share the spotlight, and allow the junior partner to grow in the practice and get increasingly involved in management. It's important that the staff learn to respect the junior partner as an owner. Management skills are learned, and this will take time, but undermining a junior partner in front of patients or staff members can be detrimental to the financial success of the practice and the relationship as a whole.

Bringing on a partner is essentially a marriage for your business. It requires communication, mutual respect, and a great prenup. In the case of a business marriage, this prenup is referred to as the *partnership agreement*. Depending on the type of entity you form, it also may be called an *operating agreement* or a *shareholders' agreement*. Regardless of what you call it, the purpose of the agreement is to ensure seamless co-ownership and management of the practice.

> **Bringing on a partner is essentially a marriage for your business. It requires communication, mutual respect, and a great prenup.**

The partnership agreement will ultimately be drafted and negotiated by your respective transactional attorneys. It will address dozens of issues, including voting rights, management responsibilities, CEO compensation, withdrawal provisions, personal guaranty requirements, matters requiring unanimous consent, deadlock provisions, drag-along rights, required chairside responsibilities . . . and the list goes on.

The most important thing you can do when negotiating a successful partnership agreement is to get into a room with your soon-to-be partner and have a conversation. You must have a real understanding of whether this relationship is going to be a good fit, and that's something your lawyer can't do for you. You must spend time with your partner to assess your compatibility. Your ability to negotiate the terms of the partnership agreement directly with your partner is the best indicator of whether this is a good fit.

There's an old expression: "People negotiate a lot more in divorce court than at the marriage altar." Successful partnerships are ones in which the negotiations start early and leave everyone satisfied with the outcome. The senior partner and the junior partner must be able to have these discussions before getting a deal done; if they can't, then they're unlikely to amicably settle any differences that arise once they become partners. How they work together on this side of the transaction is a good predictor of how well they will work as partners.

It probably comes as no surprise that the most heavily negotiated document in a buy-in transaction isn't the purchase agreement itself, but rather the partnership agreement.

Equal Partnerships

We typically advise against equal partnerships. This is because in all professional-services businesses—whether we're talking about a dental practice, a medical practice, a law firm, an engineering firm, or anything else—there must be some form of centralized leadership for the business to succeed. In my opinion, one individual must have the power to say "yea" or "nay" to keep the business running.

If you have a fifty/fifty partnership, gridlock is built into the structure. If deadlock occurs in an equal partnership, the only way to settle it is through third-party intervention (typically a judge, a mediator, or an arbitrator). Either way, partners shouldn't be in the position of taking each other to court. They should be happily running the business together.

If you don't have one individual empowered to make these decisions, then you're essentially setting yourself up for unnecessary battles down the road and, almost inevitably, an unhappy outcome: arbitration, litigation, or even the dissolution of the practice. It's important for us as attorneys to contemplate situations that the dentists don't want to think about.

No one expects that a partnership will break down. The truth is that there are a million ways for a deal to unravel, for relationships to go south, and for former friends and partners to end up as bitter enemies. By negotiating a solid partnership agreement early on, you can avoid a potential conflict, or worse, a messy divorce.

One major issue that often gives rise to these kinds of conflicts is when one partner can force a buyout of the other partner. Death, disability, and retirement are obvious triggering events, but what if your partner stops coming to work? Can you kick him out? Or what if he's the subject of a serious malpractice suit? Or a sexual harassment claim? These are issues that need to be discussed and agreed to long before problems arise.

Consider this hypothetical that's based on a true story:

Dr. Marie and Dr. Jane created a fifty/fifty partnership and decided to buy a practice together. They borrowed more than $1 million from a bank to get the deal done. Almost immediately after the closing, the partnership began to unravel. It turned out that the partners didn't know each other very well before deciding to enter into such a huge commitment together, and they ultimately didn't get along.

Dr. Marie was willing to walk away with nothing if she were to be released from the bank loan, the property lease, and the equipment loans. Dr. Marie even left the practice and moved to a different city. However, the bank refused to release Dr. Marie from the loan because it wasn't even a year old, and the practice was struggling.

Eventually, Dr. Marie hired us to help get her out of the deal. When we asked to see a copy of the partnership agreement, she gave us a one-page document. Nothing else. Dr. Marie explained that she and her partner had never discussed their partnership with the lawyer who helped them ink the deal.

Without a partnership agreement, we didn't have any leverage. Also, the bank put so many restrictions on the practice's finances, a separation of the partners became impossible. The bank required that an outside accountant maintain the books. The bank accounts were monitored and restricted, as was the compensation payable to Dr. Jane.

Essentially, Dr. Marie and Dr. Jane were forced to remain "partners" even though Dr. Marie had left the practice and moved to a different city (which was a good thing because it eliminated our need to fight over the restrictive covenant).

After six months of spinning our wheels with negotiations, we finally got everyone in a room together, and the bank proposed a compromise. Because both partners had a fifty/fifty vote, no one had the power to decide. We were at a stalemate.

In the end, the bank threatened to foreclose on the loan, which ultimately forced the partners to agree on a settlement. Without the bank making that threat, Dr. Marie and Dr. Jane would never have stopped haggling, and we wouldn't have reached an agreement.

In the end, this failed partnership cost Dr. Marie eighteen months of aggravation and more than $20,000 in legal fees.

Moral of the story: Don't buy a practice with another person until you've taken the time to negotiate a comprehensive partnership agreement. And if you insist on fifty/fifty ownership, make sure there are proper mechanisms to prevent a deadlock situation. Dr. Marie and Dr. Jane really didn't know each other well and should never have purchased the practice together, but no one took the time to sit down with them to discuss all of the issues that were involved.

Thinking through these potential problems avoids trouble down the road. No one likes to consider the possibility of failure, but having the discussion before it's relevant is easier and less painful. Wouldn't it be better to think through these uncomfortable issues in advance, before they turn into practical realities? Dispute resolution clauses, whether they point to arbitration or mediation, or naming a trusted third person as the tiebreaker, may not be enjoyable to think about before getting a deal done. However, if you ever need these tools, you'll be thankful to the team that had the foresight to take care of these issues when they were still hypothetical.

I want to conclude by reminding you what President Ronald Reagan used to say about arms-control negotiations with the Soviets: "Trust, but verify." Do your homework. Think through the serious issues—financial, cultural, and psychological.

Just as you can never predict with certainty which marriages are going to last, it's impossible to say with absolute certainty that a business partnership will work out. Most of the time, they *do* work out, but all parties must take the time to think through the difficult issues and have the hard conversations that this sort of change in a relationship requires. If you're willing to do that, and you both go into it in good faith and with eyes open, then in my experience, things will likely go well.

CHAPTER 7

DOING DEALS WITH DSOS

You have to think anyway, so why not think big?

—Donald Trump

The trend in dentistry—and throughout medicine and business in general—is consolidation, often through private equity investment. Although it's still possible for an individual dentist to successfully run an office independent of any greater corporate structure, today, private equity is recognizing the value of combining dental practices to create economies of scale and generate greater wealth for all concerned as well as a solid return on their investment.

In this chapter, we're going to examine the phenomenon of DSOs and see whether it makes sense for you to sell your practice to one, or even create a DSO for yourself.

The primary benefit of selling your practice to a DSO is that they often pay higher purchase prices than a traditional buyer. We've seen in previous chapters that DSOs, flush with cash, are ignoring prior valuation models and offering higher prices for successful dental practices. This is good news for the dentist whose practice would be attractive to a DSO. Dental service organizations prefer high-volume general-dentistry practices that accept a range of quality insurance policies, as well as high-end, cash-based practices and specialty practices. They are generally not interested in Medicaid practices unless those practices are unusually profitable. (To be clear, some DSOs are interested in Medicaid practices, but many aren't.)

Once your dental enterprise reaches a certain size, DSOs often become the only plausible buyer. This is regularly the case for multi-practice deals in which a single dentist owns several offices with gross revenue in excess of $5 million per year. Such practices are almost always out of the reach of a young dentist looking to buy a practice for himself. He's likely unable to secure bank financing for a practice of that magnitude, and he may not have the managerial experience to successfully lead such an enterprise. If you've built up a sizeable entrepreneurial empire, selling to a DSO may well be the way to go.

If you've built up a sizeable entrepreneurial empire, selling to a DSO may well be the way to go.

The tremendous explosion of DSOs in the marketplace began when private equity investors saw that they could get a great return on investment in dentistry but ran into legal restrictions because of regulations limiting the corporate practice of dentistry in many states. These restrictions stipulate that non-dentists cannot own an interest in a dental practice. Thus, the DSO became the vehicle, allowing non-licensed investors to get into the business of dentistry. A DSO is a general business entity with a fairly complex structure, the details of which are beyond the scope of this book. Suffice it to say that the DSO model is how private equity and other non-licensed investor groups can buy up multiple dental practices while still acting within the permissible scope of the law.

What to Expect When You Transition to a DSO

When you sell to a DSO, the transition can take a few years. Many DSOs will require a selling doctor to take 20 to 30 percent of the sale price in what we call *rollover equity*, which is essentially an equity interest in the acquiring company (the DSO itself). This way, the selling dentist is incentivized to participate in the post-closing success and growth of that practice.

Why is this? The DSO wants to ensure, to the extent possible, that the practice will be successful after the closing. As we discussed in Chapter 5, a smooth transfer of patient and staff relationships often requires a long transition period. Most DSOs expect relatively long-term employment agreements with the sellers and their key employees. If you're planning to sell to a DSO, you should expect that the DSO will be looking for a three- to five-year employment contract after closing. These deals are profitable, but often require a long-term commitment.

The primary scenario in which a DSO wouldn't expect the selling dentist to sign a long-term employment contract is one in which the seller can prove, to the absolute satisfaction of the DSO, that all she's been doing for the last few years is managing the practice. If you can demonstrate conclusively that your role is more CEO-like and that you haven't been treating patients, the DSO may not require a long-term employment contract.

Is it possible to stay on for fewer than three years when a DSO buys your practice? In some cases, yes. We recently represented an older dentist who sold his practice to a DSO and will only remain in the office for eighteen months. That's the shortest post-closing DSO employment contract I've ever seen for any dentist who still works chairside. However, this case is unusual. If you're going to sell to a DSO, they'll almost certainly expect you to be there longer.

Keep in mind that bigger DSOs own dozens, if not hundreds, of dental practices. The simple truth is that they don't want to be forced to staff every office that they acquire. The DSO model requires that the dentists and the staff members remain in place post-closing. The DSO is focused on the continuation of cash flow and return on investment.

Can You Create Your Own DSO?

If you're an entrepreneurial dentist and you're wondering if you have what it takes to create your own DSO, the answer is a resounding "yes!" Plenty of dentists are indeed creating their own DSOs or equivalent affiliation groups. These savvy dentist entrepreneurs are able to operate in multiple locations, enjoy economies of scale, and ultimately build something that, if they wish, could be sold for a high price to a larger DSO down the road. The rule of thumb: the larger the EBITDA (earnings before interest, taxes, depreciation, and amortization), the greater the multiple.

How lucrative is it to create your own DSO? We've seen some dentists actually roll up as many as ten, twenty, or even thirty practices into a single entity across a given geographical region. As you can imagine, such entities are highly coveted by DSOs. If you're capable of getting four or five times multiple on your annual gross income when selling a single practice, you may be able to get ten times multiple when selling a package of practices.

We've helped many dentists establish DSOs of their own, which allowed them to take advantage of outside investors. This provided equity to non-dentist partners and developed benefits, including centralized billing, a centralized call center, consolidated payroll, better insurance reimbursement rates, less expensive dental equipment and supplies, savings on employee benefit plans, and many other economies of scale. It stands to reason that you can get a better deal with Cigna or Delta if you're billing $5 million or $10 million each year, compared with an individual practice billing $2 million or less.

Similarly, DSOs can also offer sophisticated real estate management services, equipment leasing, marketing, advertising, and even training. These economies of scale are hard to beat, and this is why you see consolidation.

Another benefit of creating a DSO is potential access to high-level management. The owner of a DSO will often have a chief financial officer, a director of marketing, a chief technology officer, and other C-suite officers—sophisticated professionals whom the typical solo practitioner could never afford to hire. If you have just one or two dental practices, you likely don't have the resources to layer these non-clinical salaries into your budget. However, if you're operating fifty practices, centralizing services, and getting meaningful price reductions and better insurance terms, you can now afford top-notch individuals who can run that DSO in a highly efficient and professional manner. DSOs thus allow successful practices to become even more successful because they offer a sophisticated layer of management and infrastructure that the individual practitioner simply cannot afford.

I want to emphasize that not every dentist who wants to acquire other practices needs to establish a DSO to do so. There are many ways that an experienced and creative law firm can help the entrepreneurial dentist succeed, whether with a DSO-like model or not. Different clients have different needs and styles. Whether we create an actual DSO for our client or create some other type of entity that allows for the affiliation of multiple practices, any dentist can benefit from DSO-type management and can grow the value of multiple practices, making for an even more lucrative exit down the road.

I understand that many individual practitioners see DSOs as the enemy. The truth, however, is that DSOs (and affiliations that offer some of the benefits of DSOs) create exciting new opportunities for dentists. Rather than thinking of them as a threat to the profession, it makes sense to consider how they can benefit your practice, or better yet, how you can learn from them and perhaps beat them at their own game.

The Right Representation

A word of caution: very few attorneys have substantial experience working with DSOs. You should also take into consideration that when you're dealing with private equity, you're going to be dealing with top-tier law firms and accounting firms; the contracts involved are very sophisticated. Dental service organizations usually have large national or global law firms representing them, and for their accounting needs, they often turn to the Big Four or large regional firms. So, as you can imagine, there's somewhat of a power imbalance when one of the top law firms in the United States drops a fifty-page purchase agreement onto the desk of an attorney who primarily does trust and estate work or real estate closings, and maybe some small-time litigation.

It's hardly an exaggeration to say that your financial future is riding on the outcome of this transaction. This isn't the time to have your brother-in-law do the deal for you. You must have a full-service law firm with considerable experience in these matters, one that's comfortable going up against these top firms. You shouldn't sign whatever is put in front of you, and you shouldn't be represented by attorneys who are out of their league. Will you pay more for the kind of legal representation you really need when dealing with a DSO? Absolutely. As we discussed in the due diligence chapter, the cost of hiring the right professionals to guide you through this once-in-a-lifetime transaction will be far less than paying for mistakes made if you don't assemble a competent team.

> **You shouldn't sign whatever is put in front of you, and you shouldn't be represented by attorneys who are out of their league.**

Private equity groups have fleets of people working for them. In addition to the big law and accounting firms, they've also got people on the inside—logistics people, operations people, technology people, and so on. They're all going to be calling the seller on a daily basis, asking for additional documentation. Your $5-million-a-year dental practice will go through the same rigorous analysis as a $100 million industrial company. That's why you need high-end, sophisticated counsel. Otherwise, your attorney is likely to be worn down by the bombardment of requests and more intensive due diligence than he or she has ever experienced.

I warn clients about this phenomenon all the time. I call it *deal fatigue*—the exhaustion of dealing with so many sophisticated professionals constantly asking questions and demanding more and more information over a sixty- to ninety-day period. All too often, both an attorney and a dentist unaccustomed to this level of scrutiny simply get worn down by the process and end up wanting to concede on issues where there is an unacceptable shift of risk or exposure. This often results in an agreement that is unfair to the seller.

When people come to us intent on doing a deal with a DSO, one of our biggest challenges is explaining why our services require the fees we charge. When people ask, "How much is it going to cost for you to represent me?" it's impossible to quote a fee instantly, because every case is different. Of course, if the dentist calls his buddy from the Rotary Club who typically represents home buyers, that attorney might say, "I'll do it for $5,000." In reality, you can't even do the disclosure schedules required by a DSO for $5,000. The bottom line is that you'll pay higher fees to a sophisticated firm that knows how to do these transactions properly. The downside of going to someone who isn't versed in these matters will be huge; you'll end up losing far more money in the transaction than you would've paid in professional fees.

One final note on this topic: if the attorney who represents you in the DSO matter is primarily a litigator, he's likely to approach your purchase agreement with the mentality of a litigator. Remember, as we discussed earlier, some attorneys are primarily litigators, and others are primarily focused on business transactions. Right now, you're trying to make a deal, not trying to stick it to the other side. Everybody has to feel like they've gained something for this kind of contract to be successful, so if your attorney is primarily litigation-minded, in my opinion, you're creating a huge stumbling block to getting the deal done the right way.

Transactional lawyers are experts at closing deals. We understand that the ultimate goal is getting to the closing table with happy clients on both sides. Choosing the right lawyer means getting a better deal and getting the deal done.

Also, keep in mind that each state has different licensing requirements, different regulations governing who can own a DSO, and so on. For example, in certain states, a DSO can't own clinical equipment; only the practice can own it. Because the rules are so state-specific, doing it right means working with someone who understands the ins and outs of your state's laws and has a national practice.

Life after a DSO Sale

Now that we've seen what DSOs are all about, let's talk briefly about the transition period that follows the sale of your practice to a DSO. For the most part, DSOs want business as usual; they want you to keep coming to work every day, continue managing your staff exactly as you did, and keep taking care of patients in the same manner you always have. Little by little, they'll incorporate systems that'll endeavor to make your practice more successful and more profitable. They'll also provide training and other services to aid your growth. But in the beginning, they typically don't want much to change. They want their investment to be profitable, and that means they want you and your staff to perform as before, without disruption, and without any bumps in the road. For the most part, selling dentists want to preserve their autonomy, and DSOs want them to keep it.

When Not to Consider a DSO

In our experience, most dentists who've sold their practices to DSOs have been happy with them. But are DSOs right for *all* practitioners? Of course not. If you're looking for an immediate retirement, a sale to a DSO isn't for you. No DSO wants to buy the practice of a dentist who'll be gone in sixty days. If you're not amenable to working with an entity that'll be making decisions about your practice, a DSO is probably a poor fit. If you're not prepared to do your own due diligence on the DSO, then don't get started on this path.

A lot of fly-by-night DSOs have appeared over the last five to ten years, so you have to be prepared to do the same homework on the DSO that the DSO is going to do on your practice.

The process is surprisingly simple. Start by talking to other doctors who've already been acquired by the DSO you're targeting. Ask lots of questions. Know whom you're getting into bed with before you do a transaction. This is also an area where a more experienced law firm can help you because the top firms know which DSOs are poor business partners and which are legitimate options.

It also doesn't hurt for the firm representing you to have sold other dental practices to the DSO you're planning to do business with; this means your attorneys will be familiar with the inner workings of that DSO and its legal and professional teams. They'll know whether you're dealing with a legitimate DSO that can really get the necessary funding and what you can expect at every stage of the negotiation.

It's true, of course, that the marketplace is changing and will only continue to change as time goes on. At the same time, it's essential for dentists to remember that there'll always be plenty of room for private practice, individual dental practices, and independent practitioners. This model isn't going away. You can still be successful as a stand-alone practice, despite changes in the landscape. Even if you don't want to join a DSO, you may want to consider the elements that make DSOs successful, and work with your attorney, practice management coach, and business advisors to apply those approaches to your practice.

Summing It Up

To sum things up, if you run a high-revenue practice, and you're willing to invest a few more years as the face of that practice, a deal with a DSO can be a fantastic opportunity. In nearly every DSO transaction we've handled, the sellers have been happy with their choice to sell to a DSO. You want to make sure that you're choosing the right DSO and that you're choosing the right firm to represent you. If you do things correctly, a DSO can provide a sizeable profit and an excellent exit strategy.

CHAPTER 8

A SOBERING LOOK AT WHAT CAN GO WRONG

*You must learn from the mistakes of others; you will never
live long enough to make them all yourself.*

—Anonymous

So far, we've stressed two themes in this book. One is that you must do your homework and pay attention to the details so you can buy, sell, or merge a practice with excellent financial results for everyone involved. The other is that you must understand the importance of legal representation by professionals who are familiar with these types of transactions.

Now, I want to share some of the worst horror stories our firm has encountered. I want to show you what can go horribly wrong. If all this book does is keep you from signing a boilerplate purchase agreement, I'll have done my job. If you take away nothing else, remember that having a solidly drafted agreement is a prerequisite for your future financial success.

First in, First Out Woes

Let me start with the unhappy case of a dentist I'll call "Dr. Sarah," who borrowed more than $1 million to buy the practice of a dentist I'll call "Dr. Jeff." Dr. Sarah really didn't consider what it'd be like to work side by side with Dr. Jeff, who had an ego the size of Texas. As in other situations we've discussed in earlier chapters, Dr. Jeff undercut Dr. Sarah at every turn, telling patients that her recommended treatment plans were foolish and a waste of money, bad-mouthing her to the staff, and otherwise making her life miserable.

As unhappy as Dr. Sarah was coming to the practice day after day, Dr. Jeff's pettiness was the least of her problems. The real issue was that her attorney had failed to pay attention to the all-important issue of accounts receivable. It isn't uncommon for patients to have outstanding bills for past treatment while continuing to be treated at the practice.

A common question that comes up in every deal we work on is, "Who keeps the preclosing accounts receivable that are collected after closing?" Generally, the accounts receivable are paid to the seller. A savvy attorney will always negotiate a good deal, whether she represents the buyer or the seller. In this case, the attorney who represented Dr. Sarah (not an affiliate of our firm) allowed Dr. Jeff's attorney to insert a "first in, first out" clause. This meant that when a patient had an outstanding invoice for prior work, every dollar that came into the practice after closing went to Dr. Jeff until his old balances were paid off. A patient may come in for a crown but owe money for a different treatment from last year. When that patient makes a payment, the agreement required that the money be paid to Dr. Jeff.

Under normal circumstances, when accounts receivable are kept at a reasonable level, a "first in, first out" clause doesn't present a huge issue. However, in this particular case, Dr. Jeff's receivables at the time of closing were more than $400,000! That's 40 percent of the practice's sale price.

As you can imagine, this crippled Dr. Sarah's cash flow, making the practice all but impossible to maintain. She could barely pay the practice's expenses, and she also had to make installments on that $1 million bank loan.

Dr. Sarah brought us in, and we were able to get Dr. Jeff fired for insubordination. This made her life easier on a day-to-day basis, but it didn't address the accounts receivable problem. Dr. Jeff still managed to get a substantial portion of the fees that came into the practice. This was so destructive to Dr. Sarah's finances, she ended up having to file for bankruptcy. All of this could have been avoided if her previous attorney thought through the accounts receivable issue and put a clause into the agreement giving Dr. Sarah the right to fire Dr. Jeff.

No Restrictive Covenants? No Good.

Here's another sad story, which also could've been prevented had the original attorney been familiar with the issues surrounding the purchase of a dental practice. Our client, Dr. Joe, purchased a practice from Dr. Norm. Dr. Joe was represented by a family friend with no dental practice transaction experience. The issue in this case was Dr. Alice, the one associate working in Dr. Norm's practice. Dr.

Norm himself was an absentee owner by the time of the sale, and Dr. Alice was performing all of the procedures at the practice.

Two months after Dr. Joe purchased Dr. Norm's practice, Dr. Alice quit and opened her own practice across the street. We later learned that she'd even been working on and building her new practice while still working for Dr. Norm.

Although the agreement had a restriction on the seller, there were no restrictions on his associate, so there was absolutely nothing stopping Dr. Alice from taking all of the patients from Dr. Joe and treating them across the street at her new practice. Within months of closing, the value of Dr. Joe's practice plummeted. Dr. Alice essentially took the practice for nothing after Dr. Joe had borrowed half a million dollars to purchase it.

Dr. Joe asked me to review the situation, but by the time he came to us, there was little we could do for him. Dr. Joe's previous attorney hadn't insisted that the associate enter into either an employment agreement or a restrictive covenant agreement as a condition to the closing. Instead, Dr. Joe and Dr. Norm committed to everything on a handshake, so nothing in the written agreement prohibited Dr. Alice from competing or soliciting the patients. As unfair as it was, Dr. Alice had every legal right to do what she did.

I Hate to Say "I Told You So"

Here's a situation in which we were the attorneys representing the buyer, and the deal didn't pass the smell test—but we were unable to convince the buyer not to buy.

Dr. Pete owned two practices, one in the city where he lived, and one just outside the city. He wanted to sell the suburban practice to our client, Dr. Alex, but every time we asked for financial information, it'd come in slowly, in bits and pieces. Trying to get any real information out of the seller was torture. This is always a red flag for me; if you don't have anything to hide, why not just present the information in a complete and businesslike manner?

If you don't have anything to hide, why not just present the information in a complete and businesslike manner?

I was also concerned that the seller didn't want to make representations regarding whether patients were treated in both locations. Why not? In my career, I've seen plenty of cases in which doctors who own multiple practices comingle funds from those practices. Sometimes the bookkeeping is straightforward, and sometimes they act as though they have something to hide.

I said to Dr. Alex, "Why do you want to buy this practice? Things just don't seem right here."

He said he really wanted to close. I asked if he'd be willing to have a forensic accountant specializing in medical and dental practices dig deep into the numbers and conduct detailed patient-chart audits to see what was going on. But he refused to spend the extra money and insinuated the deal was so good, it was worth the risk to him.

So, the deal closed, and sure enough, it turned out that Dr. Pete had been pumping up the value of the practice by claiming that patients from his big-city practice were actually patients at the suburban practice—but they weren't.

There's no point in hiring a lawyer if you're going to ignore all the warning signs and advice. We advised our client not to buy that practice, but although our job is to advocate for our clients and to represent their interests zealously, that doesn't give us the right to step in and say,

"I'm not letting you do this deal." The bottom line is, listen to your attorney, and do your homework. Beware of the multi-practice seller whose financials seem suspicious. In this case, the client was defrauded because he ignored a problem we'd specifically told him to watch out for.

Poorly Managed Mergers

Next, we have a tale of two dentists, Dr. Serena and Dr. Angelo, who decided to merge their practices. The deal went through fairly smoothly. Unfortunately, Dr. Serena, whom we represented, had no idea how many problem patients Dr. Angelo was bringing into the new practice—and these people were demanding that Dr. Serena resolve problems that Dr. Angelo had caused. It was as if the floodgates had opened. Within a month, Dr. Serena's office was overwhelmed with patients from Dr. Angelo's former practice who demanded their dental work be fixed or completed immediately . . . for free.

The two dentists had to negotiate a "divorce" to get Dr. Serena away from this flood of unhappy patients. The only saving grace here was that the problem revealed itself so quickly. As with a married couple, it's a lot easier to get a divorce if the problems surface early in the relationship.

This situation reminded us of an important lesson: Always put clear breakup language in the merger agreement in case the "marriage" doesn't work out. That's a lesson we learned over the years, and our clients have benefited from that hard-won knowledge ever since.

Along those lines, we recently negotiated a merger agreement between two neighboring practices. The problem was that one of the dentists didn't want to sign a non-compete because if the deal went south, she didn't want to find herself unable to practice dentistry in her community for many years. The deal seemed stuck until we introduced a clause that allowed her to undo the deal if she became unhappy within the first twelve months. In such a case, she would have the right to leave and open a practice anywhere, without violating the non-compete, as long as she returned the purchase payment. They agreed, and the deal went through. Sometimes you have to get creative to handle a potential deal-killer.

Fifty/Fifty Profits without Fifty/Fifty Effort

In another case, two junior partners bought out their senior partner, leaving each junior partner with 50 percent of the practice. One of the partners worked excessively long hours, seeing patients constantly, managing the business, handling the marketing, and so forth. The other partner? He was nowhere to be found, yet he was still entitled to 50 percent of the successful practice's net profits. I said earlier that I don't like fifty/fifty splits because there has to be someone who can make the decisions and assume the role of managing partner. In this case, the partner who was doing most of the work had no real recourse against the partner who was shirking his responsibilities. Unfortunately, this case wound up in a dispute and resulted in the hardworking partner paying an enormous buyout price to get his partner out of the practice.

They're Not All Horror Stories

Sometimes situations that look dire can be worked out with a little creativity. Dr. Ben built a very successful practice, but he was nearing retirement age. He reached a point where he suffered from a serious medical condition that made it difficult for him to practice. In a situation like this, if you don't sell the practice quickly, the value drops drastically. If Dr. Ben were to die, become disabled, or retire, all of his patients would immediately go somewhere else.

He found a buyer, Dr. Jane, and we drafted the contracts with the intent of closing five days later. Then, trouble arose. When we did the standard lien searches, we discovered an IRS tax lien, which meant that Dr. Ben didn't have the legal right to sell the practice!

We went to the IRS and explained the situation. "No problem," they told us. "We'll expedite this and have an answer for you in two months." Two months?!

Of course, within those two months, all of Dr. Ben's patients would be gone. So, we came up with a creative solution. Instead of selling the practice, we agreed that it'd be *managed* as if Dr. Jane essentially owned her own mini-DSO. The terms made clear that once the IRS lien issue was resolved, the deal would convert from a management agreement to a standard practice sale. Dr. Jane preserved and grew the practice, realizing the profits, and months later, when the IRS lien was cleared, she closed the deal, and Dr. Ben was paid. Once again, a little bit of creativity saved the day.

Earlier in this chapter, I told you a story about the importance of including a "divorce" clause to illustrate that no firm—even ours—is perfect. It's simply impossible to insure against every possible negative outcome that you can dream up. But in these kinds of complex transactions—buying, selling, and merging practices—forewarned is forearmed.

It'd be tragic if you've read these horror stories and have concluded that dental practice deals typically go south. Nothing could be further from the truth. Most of the time, they work, and the results are advantageous for all involved. My hope is that you'll take seriously the ramifications of what may well be the biggest financial decision of your career. When it's done correctly, everybody wins, and you'll have financial and/or career security for a lifetime.

Don't let enthusiasm, impatience, or overreliance on the assertions of the other side cause you to rush into what ultimately turns into a bad deal. Take your time, conduct your due diligence, follow the advice of your attorneys—after all, that's what you're paying them for—and think things through. If you do this, you're almost certain to have a great outcome.

CHAPTER 9

IT'S TIME TO TAKE ACTION

The way to get started is to quit talking and start doing.

—Walt Disney

My father had an incredible entrepreneurial spirit. He loved talking about business and was always interested in discussing potential new opportunities. From an early age, I can remember driving around with my dad and listening to Zig Ziglar. He'd play the same cassette tapes over and over until we could all recite them by heart. Like Zig, my father's passions in life were loving his family, helping others, and succeeding in business.

When my father passed away, he left me with many gifts, including a strong set of core values. To this day, I pride myself on being a good husband and father, helping people achieve their goals, and succeeding in business. Although I ultimately decided to become an attorney, my father's passion for business wasn't lost on me. I've invested in many entrepreneurial opportunities, including some that were successful and others that weren't.

I sincerely believe that my experiences as an entrepreneur made me a better corporate attorney. Those experiences also gave me a better understanding of what it feels like to sit at the closing table, both as a buyer and as a seller. The reality is, there's no such thing as a sure thing. But in the words of the great, ever-inspiring Zig Ziglar, "What you do today can change all the tomorrows of your life."

My goal in writing this book was to demonstrate that, when properly structured, the sale of a dental practice can be an extremely lucrative and joyous event for all involved. This is an opportunity for everyone's dreams to come true.

The sale of a dental practice can be an extremely lucrative and joyous event for all involved.

If you're selling your practice, you've likely spent many years developing relationships with your patients, training your staff, and building a successful business. You've spent countless hours practicing dentistry, and it's now time to embark on the next chapter of your life. It's time to realize the financial reward of a lifetime of hard work. It's time to appreciate the legacy you've created.

If you're buying a practice, this is such an exciting opportunity. You've taken the time to hone your craft, and you're likely quite confident in those skills. However, becoming an entrepreneur requires a completely different set of skills. You aren't only responsible for keeping your patients happy, but now you also need to worry about making payroll and rent. Transitioning from practitioner to business owner is a huge step in your career, and to be honest, it can be a bit of an emotional roller coaster.

Although investing in a business can be scary, it brings with it the possibility of a lucrative financial future. There are few accomplishments more fulfilling than the ability to financially support yourself, your family, your staff, and their families.

Dentists have become increasingly entrepreneurial. They're encouraged by banks—through high-octane lending practices—to buy up practices, to sell to DSOs, or to become DSOs themselves. There's never been a better time to be a dentist with entrepreneurial ambition.

The real issue is whether you have the patience and wisdom to do things the right way. Doing it the right way means giving yourself the proper amount of time to conduct due diligence. It means hiring the right group of professionals to guide you through the process and prevent you from making costly mistakes. It means sitting down in a room and talking to the person on the other side of the table. It means having the integrity to negotiate terms that benefit both parties. It means knowing the business better than anyone else in the room.

> For many of our clients, the financial success they realize through these transactions exceeds their wildest dreams, and we love being part of that experience.

I hope this book has answered all your questions, and you now feel ready to proceed with buying, selling, or merging your practice. I hope this book has helped you understand the potential red flags and pitfalls of participating in a dental practice transaction but also brought to light the exciting possibilities available to those who have the ambition, drive, and vision to become a dental entrepreneur. I hope you now have the confidence needed to take the next step in your career. Now, it's time to take action.

ABOUT MANDELBAUM BARRETT PC

Since its founding in 1930, Mandelbaum Barrett PC has been committed to providing clients with the highest level of personal, hands-on attention for their legal needs. The firm takes a proactive approach in representing its clients from the boardroom to the courtroom. Mandelbaum Barrett PC attorneys are zealous advocates who take the time to get to know their clients.

The firm's diverse business clients include organizations of all sizes in various industries with national and international interests such as banks, governmental entities, real estate developers, public and private institutions, biotech companies, manufacturers, and health care providers and facilities, as well as individuals and families.

Mandelbaum Barrett PC is proud of its rich history but is focused on being at the cutting edge of legal innovation. The firm has continuously grown and expanded its practice areas to respond to clients' increasingly complex business and personal legal needs. Recognized as a premiere full-service law firm, Mandelbaum Barrett PC represents clients in an array of specialties, including health care business transactions, real estate, leasing, land use, business litigation and employment litigation defense, corporate and banking transactions, corporate and personal taxation, dental and medical health care and life sciences, intellectual property, privacy and cybersecurity, bankruptcy, environmental law, criminal defense, not-for-profits, and personal matters including estate planning and administration, asset protection planning, elder care, matrimonial, family law, adoptions, and personal injury litigation.

Mandelbaum Barrett PC is proud to have been selected by *U.S. News & World Report* as one of the "Best Law Firms" in 2017, 2018, and 2019.

ABOUT THE AUTHORS

WILLIAM S. BARRETT, ESQ. is the CEO of Mandelbaum Barrett PC He has over twenty years of experience representing a wide range of businesses, with a unique specialty in mergers and acquisitions, start-ups, commercial finance, and real estate transactions. He provides strategic advice to businesses of all sizes from formation to dissolution and every stage in between. He is known for the personal attention that he gives his clients and the energy he brings to every deal. Bill has a reputation as a thought leader and deal maker who knows how to get things done.

Bill began his career at one of the largest global law firms in the world, headquartered in New York City. After joining Mandelbaum Barrett PC in 1999, he was inspired to create a National Dental Law Group at Mandelbaum Barrett PC, with the objective of setting the standard for the legal representation of dentists and dental specialists in practice transitions.

The Dental Law Center at Mandelbaum Barrett PC employs the country's leading dental transaction experts and is proud to serve dentists and dental specialists nationwide.

Bill is well recognized as a dental transactional attorney, with expertise in practice sales and purchases, associate buy-ins, start-ups, and the structuring of management services organizations. He is well versed in the rules and regulations that govern the profession, with particular expertise in the health care regulations governing corporate dentistry and medicine. Bill has written many articles addressing the legal and business needs of licensed professionals and regularly speaks on a wide variety of topics to conventions, trade shows, study groups, and societies, as well as students and residents at dental and medical schools.

Bill is a proud member of the Board of Directors of Fortune Management, the nation's largest practice management consulting organization. The organization is committed to helping doctors balance practice management and personal development to create an extraordinary practice and life for the people who work within the profession and for the patients they serve.

When Bill is not serving his clients, he enjoys coaching youth sports, fishing, skiing, and traveling with his wife, Jen, and his two children, Julia and Billy. Bill resides in Mountain Lakes, New Jersey.

CASEY GOCEL, ESQ., joined Mandelbaum Barrett PC in 2008 after completing her master's in tax law at New York University School of Law. She quickly became the youngest female partner in the firm's history and was subsequently elected to the firm's executive committee.

As the co-chair of the firm's National Dental Law Group at Mandelbaum Barrett PC, Casey uses her unique blend of entrepreneurial spirit, legal expertise, and business acumen to help dentists navigate through practice transitions, corporate transactions, tax issues, and estate planning concerns. In addition to bringing deep expertise to every situation, she is widely recognized as one of the dental industry's most prolific attorneys, regularly spearheading more than fifty transactions each year.

Casey has been named a Top 50 Woman in Business, as well as a Top 25 Intrapreneur. Earlier in her career, Casey was also named one of *NJBiz's* "Forty under 40" for her commitment to professional excellence and community service, one of the "New Leaders of the Bar," and a "Rising Star" by Thomson Reuters' Super Lawyers.

Casey lives in Parsippany, New Jersey, with her husband, Dan, and her daughters Denali and Magnolia.

BIBLIOGRAPHY

Stoltz, Bernie, and Mark Murphy. *The Win-Win Outcome: The Dealmaker's Guide to Buying and Selling Dental Practices.* San Jose, CA: Fortune Management, 2018.

Are you ready to move from chairside practitioner to dental entrepreneur?

Mandelbaum
Barrett PC

Attorneys at Law

Bill Barrett and the attorneys in our National Dental Law Group at Mandelbaum Barrett PC deliver insightful legal counsel that is built on relationships and focused on results. As the go-to law firm for the dental profession, we deliver true 360° advice that addresses every aspect of your professional life, and the personal planning issues that are closely intertwined.

Working with Bill, you get the benefit of:

» Sophisticated legal counsel that will drive your practice forward

» A strategic advisor who shares your growth-oriented mindset

» An immense trove of valuable insights, built over the course of three decades in the profession

» Pragmatic, yet creative advice that's grounded in the unique concerns of entrepreneurial dentists

Contact Bill today:
wbarrett@mblawfirm.com

NOTES

NOTES

NOTES